boyzone
our story

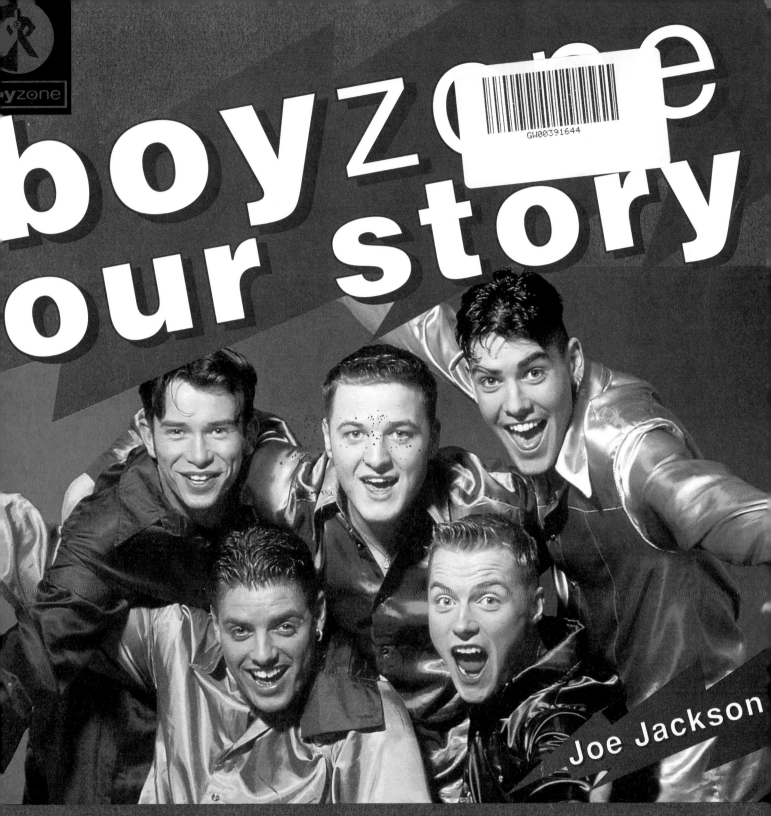

Joe Jackson

First published in Great Britain in 1995 by Boxtree Limited, Broadwall House, 21 Broadwall, London SE1 9PL

The right of Joe Jackson to be identified as author of this work has been asserted by him in accordance with the Copyright, Designs and Patents Act 1988

10 9 8 7 6 5 4 3 2 1

ISBN: 0 7522 0741 5

Design by Blackjacks, colour reproduction by Scanners

Printed and Bound in Cambus Litho Ltd, East Kilbride

A CIP catalogue entry for this book is available from the British Library

Photo Acknowledgements: Cathal Dawson: page 14; courtesy of Keith Duffy: page 24; courtesy of Steve Gately: pages 12, 13, 14 top; courtesy of Mike Graham: pages 17, 18, 19; courtesy of Ronan Keating: pages 15, 16; courtesy of Shane Lynch: page 21; Joe Jackson: pages 22, 23, 30, 34, 35, 37-50, 52-63; courtesy of Louis Walsh: pages 10, 20, 26, 61.

Special thanks to Boyzone's families who provided access to childhood photographs and to the Dublin Camera Centre and One-Hour Photo.

BOYZONE DEDICATION

One Sunday afternoon in May 1994 I was returning home, carrying in my briefcase an autographed photo of a band I'd interviewed the day before but who had yet to release their first single: Boyzone. The photo was for a neighbour, Sarah Jane Richardson, who was a Take That fanatic and whose parents, Lorraine and William, were secretly plotting with me to get her backstage to meet her idols after their forthcoming concert in Dublin. I wasn't sure if she'd heard of Boyzone but brought the picture suspecting that maybe she would be soon shifting her affections to Ireland's first bona fide teen band.

However, as I arrived at her garden gate I was told by her parents that their fourteen-year-old daughter had been knocked down by a car and was on a life-support machine. Three days later, Sarah Jane died and her parents placed in her coffin, among her most prized mementoes, a photo of Take That. "Because that's what she would have wanted", explained Lorraine. This single gesture finally, fully substantiated my belief that one should never mock or underestimate the importance of hero worship to teenage pop fans.

But then, as a person who once taught self-expression through creative writing to students in a so-called deprived area of Dublin, I had long since learned not to patronize the tastes of teenagers. How could I, without being a hypocrite? After all, as a boy, I'd been similarly besotted by Elvis Presley, and still am, to a great degree.

And so I dedicate this book to Sarah Jane Richardson and to all neophyte pop music fans who have chosen to express themselves through following bands like Take That and Boyzone. And, yes, I now am certain that Sarah would have shifted her affection to Boyzone. After all, her thirteen-year-old sister, Louise, has. And who am I to argue with that? Anything that lifts either the spirit or the voice to sing out for even a moment is surely to be applauded. And there isn't anything that lifts the spirit as much as a good pop song well sung. This, of course, brings us to Boyzone.

STEVE GATELY

Born Stephen Patrick David Gately on March 17, in Dublin. Three brothers Mark, Tony and Alan and an older sister, Michelle.

Height: 5ft. 7in.

Nickname: Homeboy, because he gets homesick every time he leaves Ireland.

Earliest Childhood Memory: A sweet shop that my friend's mother owned. I was in there all the time when I was really young!

Hobbies: Singing, acting, dancing.

First Love: Claims he hasn't ever been inlove.

Dream Date: Michelle Pfeiffer.

Of Pop Stars he met secretly fancies: Louise out of Eternal and Baby out of Reel 2 Reel because they're both really sexy.

First Record Bought: *If Only I Could* by Sidney Youngblood.

Fave TV Show: Home and Away.   **Fave Movie:** *Pretty Woman, Sister Act.*

Fave Singers: Michael Bolton, Mariah Carey.

Fave Group: Zig and Zag.

Most embarrassing memory: About five or six years ago I was at Mass and the collection box came around to me and I dropped it and the money went everywhere. I had to pick it up!

Greatest Fear: Drowning or burning in fire.

Best Thing About Being In Boyzone: The girls are great.

Worst Thing About Being in Boyzone: You get run down and tired because you're busy all the time.

Ambition: To be successful in life.

Describe yourself in five words: Quiet, fun, outgoing, mysterious, unpredictable.

Loves Dublin because: It has the best people in the world. They'll chat to absolutely anybody. If it talks we'll chat to it.

In five years sees himself: In Dublin, with a house overlooking the beach.

Distinguishing Feature: A tattoo of a Tasmanian devil on the hip!

RONAN KEATING

Born Ronan Patrick John Keating on March 3 1977 in Dublin.

Three brothers, Gary, Gerard, Kieran and one sister, Linda.

Nickname: Tin Tin.

Earliest Childhood Memory: Falling off my bike! It was Christmas and I got a brand new BMX. The brakes were too strong and I went right over the handlebars.

Hobbies: Running, swimming, car racing.

First Love: A girl called Georgina, about a year and a half ago.

Dream Date: Summer from *Baywatch*.

Pop Star you met you secretly fancied: Louis from Eternal! I went all weak at the knees.

First Record Bought: *Last Christmas* by Wham.

Fave TV Show: *Quantum Leap*.

Fave Movie: *The Breakfast Club*.

Fave Singers: Sting and Whitney Houston.

Fave Group: Boyzone! No, Take That!

Most Embarrassing Memory: When I was six or so I hit my dad on the back of the head with a golf club – he had to be brought to the hospital to get some stitches!

Greatest Fear: Snakes.

Best thing about being in Boyzone: Getting to Number One in Ireland.

Worst Thing About Being In Boyzone: Being away from home, not getting enough sleep and not eating properly.

Ambition: To have a successful musical career.

Describe yourself in five words: Shy, sensitive, quiet, caring and happy.

Loves Dublin because: The people!

In five years sees himself: In the music business, singing. If not in this band then with my own recording career.

Distinguishing Feature: Only self-confessed virgin in Boyzone!

MIKE GRAHAM

Born Michael Christopher Charles Graham on August 15 1972 in Dublin. Five sisters, Yvonne, Avril, Kathy, Claire and Debbie and a brother Niall.

Nickname: Bigboy.

Earliest childhood memory: Being born! Honestly! I remember being asleep, all nice and snug, then the next thing there was this bright light and a great big frying pan coming at me!

Hobbies: Singing and songwriting.

First Love: My mum.

Dream date: Claudia Schiffer.

Pop star you met you secretly fancied: All of eternal. And Kylie!

First record *De Do Do Do De Da Da Da* by the Police.

Fave TV show: *Top of the Pops.*

Fave movie: *Casablanca.*

Fave singers: Sting, Eric Clapton.

Fave Group: The Police.

Most embarrassing memory: At first year in secondary school I was an Elvis-type Pharoh in a school production of *Joseph and His Amazing Technicolor Dreamcoat* and I made a complete idiot of myself singing in an Elvis-type voice!

Greatest Fear: None!

Best thing about being in Boyzone: I've always been mad into music so now I get to do something with music all day. It's a hell of a lot easier than being a motor mechanic!

Worst thing bout being in Boyzone: I can't go to the local shopping centre to check out the talent!

Ambition: To be as good a songwriter as Gary Barlow.

Describe yourself in five words: Strong, silent, tight but fun.

Loves Dublin because: The people and the music industry!

In five years sees himself: Writing and recording songs.

Distinguishing feature: Has changed his name from Mikey to Mike because "in some European countries they were calling me Micky which is a slang word for a you-know-what!"

SHANE LYNCH

Born Shane Eamon Mark Stephen Lynch on July 26 1976 in Dublin. Six sisters: Catherine, Naomi, Keavy, Adele, Alison and Tara.

Nickname: Flirty.

Earliest childhood memory: Was when I was about three and on holidays in America. I specifically remember the hotel we were staying in and the room had connecting doors. When I opened my door there was a lady with blonde hair. I don't know why, but I remember that really clearly, probably because I got such a fright!

Hobbies: Surfing, bungee-jumping.

First Love: A girl called Gill.

Dream date: Melanie Griffiths.

Pop star you met you secretly fancied: No one!

First record bought: NWA.

Fave TV show: *Top Gear.*

Fave movie: *Point Break.*

Fave Singers: Bob Marley, Aretha Franklin.

Fave group: Public Enemy.

Most embarrassing memory: Falling flat on my face in front of a group of fans".

Greatest Fear: Girls!

Best thing about being in Boyzone: The fans! I've got some great presents from them, everything from jewellery and clothes to teddy bears.

Worst thing about being in Boyzone: I don't get to see my mates much and some fans ring at four in the morning.

Ambition: To get to the top in the music business.

Describe yourself in five words: Shy, sensitive, controlled, fearless and easy-going.

Loves Dublin because: My family.

In five years sees himself: Married! I *know* I'll be married. If this group isn't here, then I won't be in the music business at all. I'll definitely be living in Ireland.

Distinguishing feature: Tattoo of a stallion on his shoulder.

KEITH DUFFY

Born Keith Peter Thomas John Duffy on October 4 1974 in Dublin. Two brothers, Derek and John.

Nickname: Duffster.

Earliest Childhood memory: Getting a wigwam and Indian costume for Christmas. I was about four!

Hobbies: Playing the drums, singing.

First Love: My mammy.

Dream Date: Beth from *Neighbours*.

Pop star you met you secretly fancied: Michelle Gayle.

First record bought: *Slippery When Wet* by Bon Jovi.

Fave TV show: *Neighbours*.

Fave movie: *Stripes*.

Fave singers: Dickie Rock.

Fave group: East 17.

Most embarrassing memory: Trying to avoid some fans at Donaghmede shopping centre, walking into a door which had an empty pane of glass then getting home and realising I'd forgotten something, having to go back to the shops only to see the same fans again!

Greatest fear: Falling over on stage.

Best thing about being Boyzone: Getting out of doing an architecture course in college!

Worst thing about being in Boyzone: Nothing!

Ambition: To be rich and famous.

Describe yourself in five words: My bark is worse than my bite.

Loves Dublin because: The people, the culture and the home life.

In five years sees himself: Still working with the band, making lots of money!

Distinguishing feature: Is short-sighted but doesn't tell anyone in case they make him wear glasses!

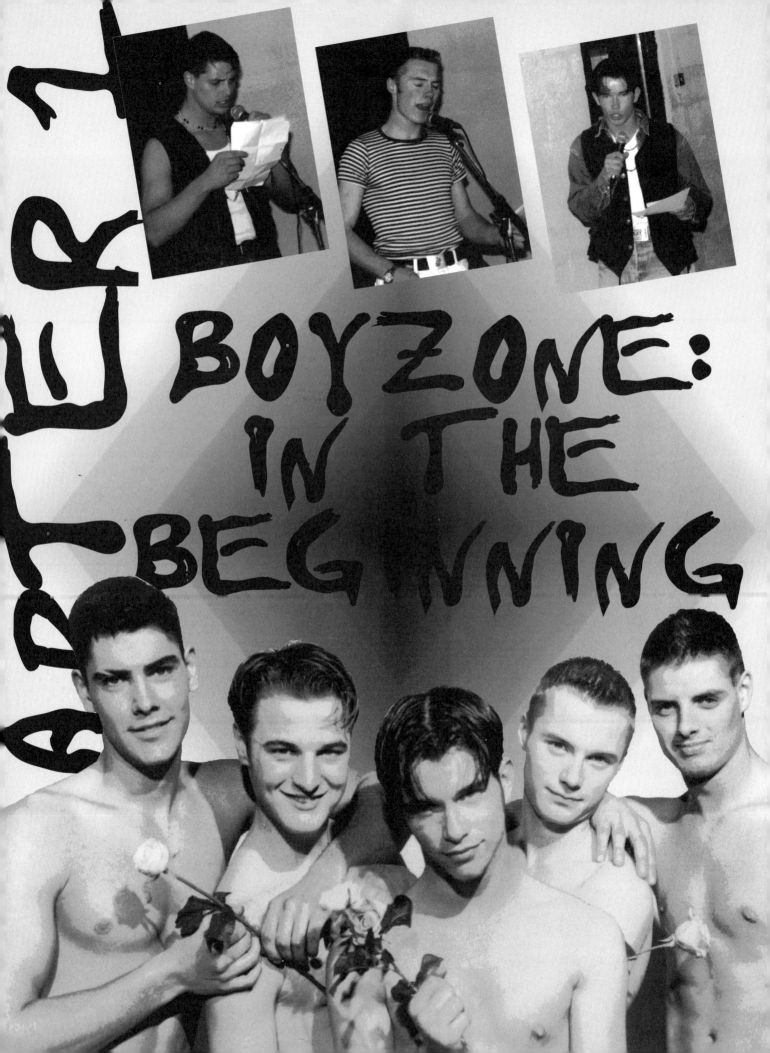

BOYZONE: IN THE BEGINNING

The date: May, 1994. The Time: early Saturday afternoon. The Place: The POD, Dublin's premier Dance club, owned by one of Boyzone's two managers, John Reynolds. Their other manager is Irish impresario Louis Walsh. Boyzone are practising in the background, singing songs such as *Every Time You Say Goodbye.* One by one they enter the deserted VIP room, all feeling slightly nervous as this is their first major interview. It also is the first time I met the guys who immediately struck me as down-to-earth and somewhat fazed by the fact that anyone from the *Irish Times would* want to interview them at all. But, like most Irish people, once given the chance to talk, they talk and talk and – well, let's flashback to that afternoon. My opening question for every member of Boyzone was: "So, like fellow Dubliner, Bob Geldof, and countless rock stars did you get into music to get rich, famous and, eh, laid?"

"Hi! I'm Steve And in answer to your question, of course I did! Why else would anyone get into the music business! And I must tell you that one thing I'm really looking forward to is being a heartthrob, the idol of thousands of girls! I read people like D-ream saying it becomes a problem when you get too famous but I've already had a taste of it and I love it! One time, in particular, I was fed ice cream in the Irish Film Centre by eight girls! They were spooning this ice cream into my mouth and I was just sitting back lapping it all up! I'd been there having a pint and two girls came in and said 'it's him, it's him' then ran off and came back with another six girls! Then they asked me what my favourite food was and I mentioned ice cream! They were around 16-18 and I got all their phone numbers! It was like being in heaven!

But I myself am 18, from Seville Place, in Dublin's inner city and my background is in dancing, because I studied dance for six years.

I also did years of voice training and acting and some modelling. Mostly because, since I was about nine, I was determined to be famous, no matter what. I just felt I had to do that because there's no one famous in my family and I said 'I'm going to be the first to be well-known throughout the world!' The same applies in terms of my street. There's no one down there who has made it and I want to be the first person who does. It's really important that I make it, coming from that area of Dublin, because I want to do the area proud. For years it's been put down as a slums, which it's not. New houses are being built there as we speak. And there is unbelievable talent down there, in terms of disco-dancing and drama.

"Yet, because of where I come from I definitely have no time for drugs at all. I used to drink more, to be social, but now I'm not pushed whether I drink or not, though I like shorts! But I've no interest in drugs like E, or whatever. I look at a lot of my friends, where I come from, and I think 'God love you!' Because if you go down my way you see

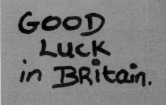

GOOD LUCK in Britain.

THOUGHT THAT WOULD MAKE YOUR DAY!

To Boyzone
Good Luck
Sure you won't need it!
Lots of Love

kids who are victims of drugs and that turns me totally against drugs. And recently I had a friend who died from heroin and no one even knew he was on it, because he was living in London. He was only 21. So I wouldn't touch drugs at all, no matter how famous we get.

"But every time I thought, 'I'm going to escape from all this' I always knew it had to be in the entertainment business, singing, acting or modelling, whatever. And all of that experience is important in Boyzone.

"And I think the same thing is going to happen big-time when Boyzone really becomes famous. I can't wait! And we *will* become famous, because of the back-up we've got and the people in the group themselves. We're all very positive and very confident and that's what keeps us going. And we really relate to each other brilliantly. We're all really good friends, but then, from the beginning, we decided there'd be no back-biting and that if you

want to say something bad about a person you say it to their face. And that's what we do! And, apart from the official meetings with John and Louis we also have meetings to discuss everything ourselves, mostly in McDonalds in Grafton Street. That's where our board meetings are held!

"Yet my dream is to be there all the time in the charts. I don't only want one, or three singles. I want hit after hit after hit! And hit albums. And I know we're going to make it. We all do."

RONAN KEATING

I'm Ronan,17, from Swords in Dublin I started out by singing in other local rock bands before all this happened. Yet I write a lot of songs and that's always been a big part of things for me. But I also was an actor and did a lot of shows, musicals and such. Yet I'm worried that people won't take the music seriously. Of course, our looks are very important too, especially when you're dealing with young kids who like to see something that looks good on stage. That's what helps sell records and that's what's important.

"But, no, this doesn't mean there's rivalry in the band and that I look at someone else and say 'I hate him because he's better looking than I am, I'm going to trip him up on stage!' We're all in this together! And what's really important is that we get on, as mates. We do gel together very well. And the point, for me, is that I don't have many friends outside the band. I've one or two close friends but that's all. And the great thing is that they're not jealous of me in any way, they're proud of me, which really makes me feel even better about all this.

What worries me is that teen bands only last, what, five years at the most? By that time, I'll only be 22 so what do I do then? Acting, I hope. Or I may go solo. What's important is that I use Boyzone to make the kind of connections that will

lead me into something else later. Because, before this, I was in school and finally had to give that up to do Boyzone because after being out with the guys working one night I just couldn't concentrate on my studies the next day. Besides, I was in another world concentrating on the band all the time. Yet I do sometimes wish I'd stayed in school and finished my Leaving Certificate exams.

"At first, my parents didn't want me to leave without doing the exams, yet finally they gave in. But that means a lot is riding on this. It has to happen for me. But I know it will. I know Boyzone will be the first pop band out of Ireland. I've no doubt about that, even though we haven't even got a single out. But we've done the single, *Working My Way Back To You,* and it's great. And we're working so hard right now to build up the whole thing, like taking dance lessons from Kylie Minogue's choreographer. It's no bed of roses in terms of the work you have to put into this and people tend not to realise that. But I feel I can meet all those demands, as in dancing well, looking good, singing, writing. In a sense I have to. My future depends on this."

MIKE GRAHAM

'I'm Mike, 21, the "daddy" of the band! And my base, in terms of music is that I've always loved music and see myself mostly as a singer/songwriter in that I play guitar and write all my own songs. I was also involved in Billy Barry's School, for dance and drama classes from the time I was five 'till I was fifteen. My family are pretty musical too, so that's where it started for me. We're all into music and singing. But it's really only meself and one of my sisters that are really strongly into it, though I am more than her because I got the inspiration to play guitar and write songs mostly from listening to

people like Eric Clapton, Sting, Paul Simon and soul-based music. That's the kind of stuff I write.

"In fact, I wrote a lot of that stuff before the band came together and now, myself and Ronan get together and try to write songs that will suit the band. And we

will, in time. We're also very aware that if you really want to make money in this business you have to write, and hold on to the publishing rights of your own songs. That's one of the main things I've picked up about the music business.

"But I've no doubt that this is what I was meant to do. All my life this is what I've been aiming for and this is my big break. And all the lads know this has to work, and that it will. It's just something we feel in out bones. I don't want to sound arrogant and pompous but this is what I am. At first I used to be very shy about saying things like that, because I hate people who are arrogant. Yet the more confident I became, in terms of my musical abilities, the more I realized I should let people know about it. Because you can keep something locked up inside yourself forever and not tell anyone about it, because you don't have the confidence. I know many Irish people like that. But more and more, we seem to be getting the kind of belief in ourselves that tells us to go for something and to tell the world about it. That's exactly what I feel like doing right now.

"A large part of it is the fact that Ireland is on the crest right now, with us winning awards all over the place. Particularly in terms of music. This country is now at a stage where the world has its eye on us, looking to see who is going to follow U2 and the Cranberries and so on. So it would be a real plus for us to produce a pop band, like Boyzone, who just might be as successful, in a similar way. That's our dream. And the lads and me are out to win. We're not out to be a one-hit wonder. What's the point, when we have the capability of being so much more?

"By trade, I'm a mechanic, because I have to survive in the meantime. Yet when I go home at night to my bedroom what I do is write music and listen to music. It really is my life. And when we get criticized by people, say, for just doing cover versions to begin with, I'll just say to myself 'Bide your time, Mike, soon they'll realise they are wrong'. People are bound to try and pull us down but I know what Boyzone is capable of and in time we'll prove ourselves. And if Boyzone falls apart I'll get into music at some level. God only knows how long this will go on for, with the lads, but when it ends I'll just move into a solo career. Music is what I love, and breathe, so I really have no choice in the matter. Now that I've gotten my break, I'm in the music business for life. First I'll get recognition with Boyzone then I'll get recognition for the music I make by myself. And to hell with the begrudgers! They don't have to listen to me, if they don't want to. And I don't have to listen to them!"

SHANE LYNCH

"Hi! I'm Shane and we're all in Boyzone to get rich, famous and laid, basically! But it's also really a good thing to do for Ireland because we haven't had a pop band like this before, so it's a dream come true for us to try that. My own dream started off with New Kids on the Block. When I was about 12 I saw them on the telly and said to myself 'I want to do that!' Then I started putting their posters on me wall, and all. Yet then I started work, as a mechanic, with me father and I was always singing around the garage, and dancing while I was working and he'd say, 'You should get into that, get it together'. He wasn't cynical at all. Though he did say I should stay working as a mechanic and do it in my spare time. Yet he gives me time off now, when I have to do things like practise and so on. He's really supportive in that way. And he gives me advice in terms of the money we're making out of this, and what we should be making. Most of the money now goes into building up Boyzone, though we get paid for certain gigs. But, in terms of contracts, I have to get a solicitor to look at mine because I'm only 17. Yet there is a contract in progress and we're waiting for that to come through. And what's always on your mind is that managers can rip people off in the music business, so you've got to keep an eye on that.

But I fairly have my head together in that respect and I think Louis and John are two good guys in this respect and hopefully they'll look after us as they should out of all this.

"But apart from the money and the girls, what really excites me is the thought that my picture just might be up there on the bedroom walls of girls and they might be looking at me saying, 'I could imagine having him!' That's what it's all about! That's what I used to think looking at pictures of Dani Minogue, or whoever! That whole idea gives me a kick. And if someone comes up to me after a gig and says she'd like to have me, we'll see what happens! But then I already have loads of girlfriends, in different nightclubs, waiting for me because of being in Boyzone! They've heard I'm in a band and you see them flock around when you're dancing! It's great! I love being the centre of attention! Who doesn't? Even when you go out you know people are looking at you, and talking and nudging each other and pointing at you! That feels good! Though maybe it's 50/50 because some people also think you're stupid. Some guys do. Like when I go to clubs some guys try to start fights because their girlfriends are into Boyzone. I'm not a fighting person, but if someone pushes it, I'll retaliate.

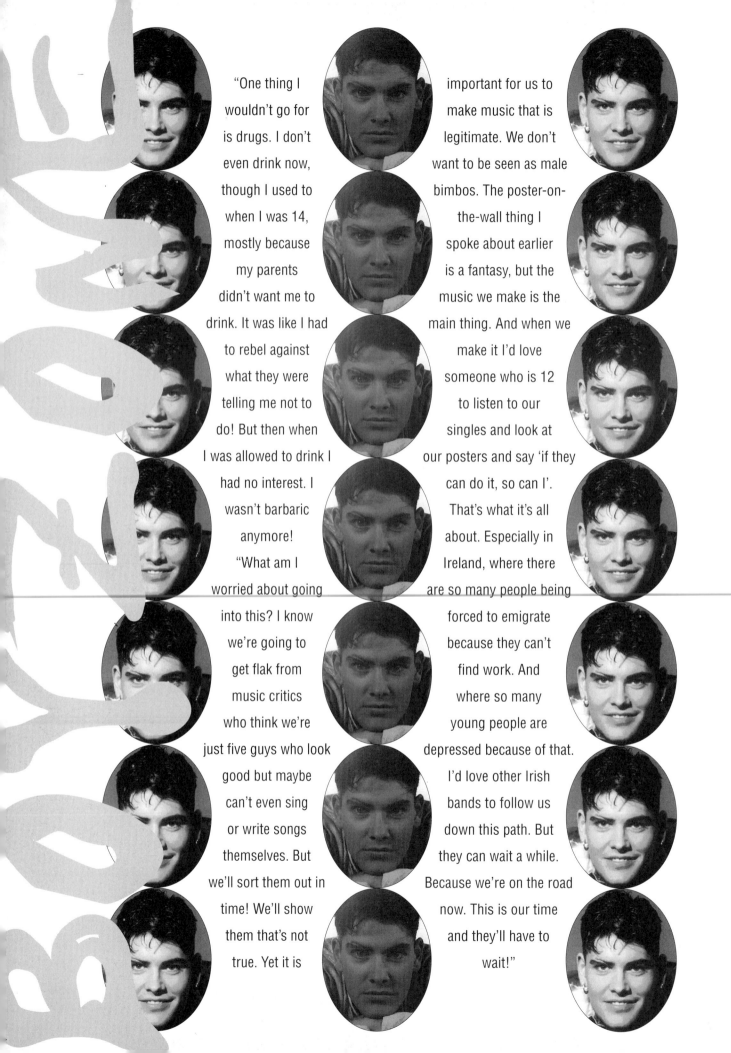

"One thing I wouldn't go for is drugs. I don't even drink now, though I used to when I was 14, mostly because my parents didn't want me to drink. It was like I had to rebel against what they were telling me not to do! But then when I was allowed to drink I had no interest. I wasn't barbaric anymore!

"What am I worried about going into this? I know we're going to get flak from music critics who think we're just five guys who look good but maybe can't even sing or write songs themselves. But we'll sort them out in time! We'll show them that's not true. Yet it is important for us to make music that is legitimate. We don't want to be seen as male bimbos. The poster-on-the-wall thing I spoke about earlier is a fantasy, but the music we make is the main thing. And when we make it I'd love someone who is 12 to listen to our singles and look at our posters and say 'if they can do it, so can I'. That's what it's all about. Especially in Ireland, where there are so many people being forced to emigrate because they can't find work. And where so many young people are depressed because of that. I'd love other Irish bands to follow us down this path. But they can wait a while. Because we're on the road now. This is our time and they'll have to wait!"

KEITH DUFFY

"I'm Keith. And, like Shane, I definitely am in this to get rich, famous and laid. I particularly like the laid part of it! Though I'm not saying I'd any problems getting laid before I joined Boyzone. It's just a lot easier now! And I mean that big time! Like last night I went home to a house in Killiney with a model I met down in Shafts nightclub and we went swimming at half six this morning! But then I'm really the only one out of the band who goes clubbing, then on to a party if I can – though I don't actually sleep with many women. I stay awake with them! But, seriously, I do believe that if you're going to start having sex with someone it means so much more if you actually are in love with that person. I'm being totally honest with you here, talking with you as one guy to another. So, no, I don't go around trying to have sex with every woman I meet. I've more respect for meself. And I didn't shag that girl last night, just had a little of this and that, if you know what I mean!

And when we go out on the road if all that becomes a part of things I'd be sure to practice safe sex and all. But what's most important to me is not how a girl looks but what's inside. You can go out with a model and maybe you both look great walking into pubs, and all, for about two months after you meet, but if you don't communicate what's it all worth, in the end? And I really do think that making love with a girl you really know is a hundred times more exciting than a quick shag. I'd rather be going out with a girl, have a steady relationship, then when you get closer and closer finally make love. That's why I imagine it's going to be hard to trust girls when we do get famous, because you won't know whether they really want to know you as you are or are just into your fame. So, maybe the best thing is to go with a girl before it all starts and then you'll always be sure it was you she wanted and not just a member of Boyzone.

"One thing I think is going to be part of it is that some guys are going to be chasing us too,

because young pop bands like Take That and all do have gay fans. But I'm not intimidated by that because I hang around in a gang with ten people and seven of them are gay. And, during the week, I hang around with guys in a flat and they're gay as well. But, if you're heterosexual they respect that and don't go near you. In fact, some gays guys have been the best friends I've ever had, and have stood by me through thick and thin. Maybe they have secret fantasies about me but they never talk about it, if they do. Maybe at the start they did, but not now. Though I think the majority of the guys in the band would be freaked out big time if gays come on to them, so we'll look out for them on that level.

"They're always warning me not to be clubbing on this night, not to be drinking on that night but, hey, you only live once! Yet I'm not allowed to go out tonight because we've got a photo session in the morning! They don't want any wrinkles under me eyes! But I'm not complaining because already it's all more exciting than I could describe. It is a dream come true.

"Before this I was in college doing architecture but, though I came top of the class in the first year, I left after two weeks after going back to college after the summer holidays. I just got totally bored by it and then worked in restaurants as a waiter and even done a bit of stripping in ladies' clubs! With a bit of luck you'd be home swimming with some of those women too, after the show! Though that whole thing was hush-hush in the beginning until the *News of the World* phoned up our house and said 'Does Keith

Duffy, the boy from Boyzone, who used to do stripping, live here?' and me Ma bawled and me Da laughed! They hadn't known about it until then. But the family are behind me a hundred per cent.

"You do need good friends to come along and tell you to keep your feet on the ground during all this stuff with Boyzone, because you really can begin to float! Ronan and Stephen are the youngest in the band and they tend to fly away now and again but I try to make sure I don't. And, despite my looks, I'm not an airhead and I'd hate to give out that impression. All of us in the band have our heads screwed on right, though people who don't know us think we're five Irish bimbos being manipulated by two managers, as happens to many bands in pop music. But that's not us at all.

"Yet I have to admit that, at the moment, I'm stone broke. Last night, I hadn't got a penny to go out, until me mates came back in. I was sitting in, on me own, waiting for them to come back. Two guys gave me twenty quid and said, 'let's go!' But I do look forward to the time when I'm making the money and I can do things like that for my friends. That's one of the reasons for becoming rich, isn't it? And I think we will become rich, because I'd trust Louis Walsh with me life. He's like a father-figure – or a mother-figure! He looks after everything. And I think he and John Reynolds, our other manager, will see to it that we're not ripped off. So, we will get rich, laid and very famous!"

CHAPTER 2 THE BIG BREAK: TOP OF THE POPS

The Date: late December, 1994. The Time. late Wednesday Afternoon. The Place: *Top of the Pops* Studio in Elstree, London. Having been in Britain doing non-stop interviews and publicity for three weeks all the members of Boyzone are feeling extremely homesick and tired. This explains their relatively muted response to this first appearance on *Top of the Pops* and to the fact that on the same day they saw a copy of the latest issue of *Smash Hits* which featured them on the cover. Working on an assignment for Irish rock magazine *Hot Press* I accompanied Boyzone on their trip to do the pre-recording of *Top of the Pops* and winged my report back to Ireland.

Love them or loathe them, when the history of Irish pop is written 1994 will probably be remembered as the year of Boyzone. Rock groups like Ash may endlessly crash into the "Indie" charts but it is these five Northside Dublin guys who this year became the first-ever Irish group to make their debut in the British Top Ten who are now are tipped to take over the top spot for Christmas, with *Love Me For A Reason*. Similarly, in Ireland their debut single *Working My Way Back To You* would have dominated the charts all summer long were it not for the phenomenal success of *Riverdance*.

And so, when Boyzone member Keith Duffy waved directly at the camera during the recent Smash Hits Poll Winners Concert in London and said, "Everybody at home – we made it!" he was obviously right.

Boyzone also occupies the cover of the current issue of the influential teen-bible *Smash Hits* photographed over a headline which reads "The Six Days That Made Them Famous! " And only the most measly-mouthed begrudger would argue against the fact that, on its own terms, this is obviously as much an achievement for the Irish music business as similar chart successes this year by the likes of Therapy? and the Cranberries.

To have moved from school, dead-end jobs and potential unemployment to now playing for more than 20,000 people at a poll-winners concert plus winning that Best New Band award within less than a year is clearly no mean feat – though cynics will claim that such a move has more to do with marketing than it has to do with music. Maybe it has. But surely the

same thing applies – to a greater or lesser extent – to most acts that break into the singles or albums charts these days, "indies" or otherwise.

The concept of "street cred" in rock is too often a myth sold by "grown-up" teen magazines like the *NME* in order to add a veneer of "artistic credibility" to its musicians. Likewise, the concept of "originality" which has already led to Boyzone being heavily criticized in certain circles because "they don't even write their own songs". So? They sing, dance and look good. Since when did these abilities fade to zero in the face of the over-rated role of composing? Besides, in Irish rock music, in particular, "originality" too often means merely mimicking bands like U2 or, more recently, the Cranberries, and covering your tracks as cleverly as possible. And while one would never argue for any inherent artistic value in Boyzone cover versions, there can be no doubt whatsoever about the validity of their music as an expression of the desire to escape from the limitations of their lives, whether they choose to describe that aspiration in rock 'n' roll terms as "getting rich, famous and laid" or otherwise.

The same applies to the thousands of teenage girls who have chosen Boyzone as the target for longings that have always been mocked in the sexist, male-dominated world of rock, since the early days of Fabian and Pat Boone. And let's not be ageist here. There are also undoubtedly many not-so-young women who want to mother, marry or romance

ragged toy boys Shane Lynch, Mike Graham, Ronan Keating, Keith Duffy and Steve Gately. Plus, of course, gays – that great, uncelebrated constituency that has always been drawn to teen idols, many of whom themselves are gay but terrified to "come out" lest that dampen the ardour of their female fans.

So where and how did it all begin for Boyzone? When, exactly, were plans set in place that have since led to Ireland's first teenybop band who now seem set to replace the likes of Take That – at least in the affections of fans of *Smash Hits* and *Top of the Pops*. Why, with *Smash Hits* and *Top of the Pops*, of course! And an addict of both, Louis Walsh, one-time manager of pop-acts like Linda Martin is now co-manager of Boyzone. His partner is John Reynolds who also owns Dublin premier dance club, the P.O.D.

"I always read *Smash Hits* and watched *Top of the Pops* and saw all those great pop groups and realised there's nothing like that in Ireland: a good looking pop band created solely for the young girls," he says, clearly eager to address the claim that his hand-picked babes are merely mini-Chippendales and nothing more.

"But although this started out simply as a marketing exercise it has grown into more because the guys really are talented musically and some of them do write their own songs and were in bands before this, so it's not a Chippendales thing" he continues. "And we picked the guys not just on their looks but for their vocal and dance abilities. There were roughly 300 we auditioned and what's important too is that they really do have to be nice guys and get on well because they're going to be travelling together in mini-buses, looking out for one another, living together and all that kind of stuff".

And, one presumes, yielding to, or battling against the excesses of pop stardom. So, what is Louis's rule in relation to Boyzone doing drugs, drinking, indulging excessively in sex?

"Drugs will damage their image and screw up their heads," he says. "Apart from that most of them don't

even drink, and anything else is their own business as long as they do it behind closed doors."

So, who's money is backing Boyzone and does Louis dream of becoming a millionaire out of all this?

"Most of the money comes from myself and John mainly, and Paul Keogh, from Polygram, who is helping us a lot. And yeah, sure, I'd like to become a millionaire out of Boyzone. And I want them to be so big in Ireland, England, Europe, America that they themselves will also make so much money that they can do what they want after this. And whatever is happening to his career now, Jason Donovan for example, did make a lot of money along the way. I think at least two of the guys in Boyzone have promise for long-term careers in the music business, Ronan and Steve. Ronan is only 17 and he's writing his own songs and Steve is just a great singer. So, who can tell what they'll do after this? They're the two who have recording contracts with Polygram. And though I know the lads are getting heavily slagged in

Ireland by so-called 'serious' rock critics they can deal with that because they know it's a knee-jerk response. What those critics forget is that there was no group in rock as manufactured as the Sex Pistols. All anybody ever compares Boyzone to is the Monkees. But they can deal with that. And so can I. There are many would-be rock stars in Dublin attacking us, but they're just begrudgers, jealous because we're making hits and they're not".

But what if Walsh becomes so ego-driven that he drives the guys into the ground, dictating work schedules that leave them looking as exhausted as they do today at *Top of The Pops* for instance? "That won't happen" he says. " Because, someone like Tom Watkins is more my role model and he's no egomaniac, though he's managed huge acts through the years from Wham to the Pet Shop Boys to East 17. I look to him for guidelines, no one else. And though I know they may be feeling like I'm running them into the ground at the moment, it has to be done while things are happening. And they really can't be complaining about this because looking back on 1994 they have to realize they are some of the luckiest guys around. I know some of them don't like the rules about not publicizing any relationships with girlfriends but that's nothing compared to the way some managers deal with teen bands, fining them if they arrive late, dictating everything they do or say to the media. They're better off than many, in this respect. And if they want to be back in Dublin with girlfriends and not over here doing things like *Top of the Pops* then they should have joined Irish rock band Aslan. In fact Boyzone are the luckiest guys I know in the music business right now".

In the meantime *Love Me For A Reason* which was made for a budget of roughly £10,000, including the cost of the video, has sold more than 60,000 copies and could conceivably sell half a million by Christmas. So how does this money break down at the moment for Boyzone? Is it true each are on a weekly salary of between £100-£200 pounds and don't see the profits

from record sales because it's all reinvested into the project?

"They get something like that, yeah," says Louis. "But they also get money for food from the record company and accommodation in London. In fact we're making enough money from gigs and appearances not to have to take anything out of the money that's been pumped back into building up the band. And every time they do a gig they get paid. Likewise, when the really big money does come in it will be all theirs. They all took individual legal advice on their contracts before signing them, which is something every band has to do these days."

John Reynolds, who admits that if he becomes a millionaire out of Boyzone "that would be great" also believes that the band needn't necessarily have a short life-span.

"If this whole thing was packaged in a way where it is more of a marketing product than a musical product then Boyzone would have no hope of longevity," he elaborates. "But there is an inherent talent there that could blossom into one of Ireland's better pop bands. They are writing some very good songs, and not just bubblegum pop but beautiful ballads. And there is a moral responsibility on myself and Louis to see that Boyzone are not exploited. Some of them are only 17, we have to look out for them in all respects. And whereas Louis deals with most of the business in relation to the guys, I probably have more of a one-to-one relationship with them so I do see all this as my responsibility."

In this context John Reynolds "totally agrees" with the "no drugs" dictate imposed on Boyzone.

"Firstly because I'm totally anti-drugs as I've seen drugs mess up too many people's lives," he says. "Secondly, on a business level, if they got into drugs it would just ebb and flow away at the whole foundation of Boyzone and the whole thing would start to crumble. The market to which Boyzone appeals is not the long-haired hippies who smoke pot, or whatever. They don't mind if one of their pop idols uses drugs, whereas Boyzone are expected to be clean-cut and must be seen to be that way."

But can the guys deal with pressures such as no drugs, not being allowed be seen with their girlfriends in public and living on a relatively average wage until the product really starts showing a profit? "Definitely", says Shane.

"You can't get success without some sacrifices. I used to drink, when I was younger. And I've no interest in drugs at all. Recently, I went to a dance with me old schoolmates and couldn't believe the amount of them that were on E. It's ridiculous, and sad. So drugs are no temptation to me at all. And in so many ways the sacrifices are worth it because I just keep remembering how I used to look at pictures of New Kids on the Block when I was 12 and think 'I want to be just like them'. That's how it started for me. But I don't want to be seen as just a male bimbo and I hope people listen to the music too."

Earlier, while standing on stage in the *Top of the Pops* studio, for the first time, Shane had looked across at PJ and Duncan on another stage and said "I can't believe we're actually here, it's brilliant". However, backstage, during a long day of rehearsals he and the other guys in Boyzone are in a more muted mood. They also are obviously nearing exhaustion and missing home on this, their fourth week in Britain doing press interviews.

replace
Take That
they themselves
will be likewise shoved
aside in time?

"Of course. All of us in
Boyzone know that. And the fact
that we've gone

"We *are*
tired," says
Shane, sighing
slightly. "Because we do
have a ridiculous schedule.
You wake up in the morning and
go 'what day is it? Where am I? What
am I supposed to do today?' And even being
here at *Top of the Pops* was hard earlier because
after telling you it was brilliant to be part of it all, the
first run-through went wrong and we all felt crap.
Neneh Cherry talked over the intro and that threw us
from the beginning. Things like that can come
crowding down on top of you."

That said, how did Shane respond to singing
before 20,000 plus people at the *Smash Hits* show?
"It was unreal, just to feel the energy coming off that
crowd made us so nervous, but we got through that
too!" he says, smiling and shaking his head.

"But the best part was there really is this sense that
Take That and some of the others are coming to the
end of their run and we're moving in. Lots of people
were saying that. Because we are new and fresh,
whereas Take That are old and worn out. They've had
their time and people are bored seeing their faces in
magazines like *Smash Hits*. They're looking for new
faces and seem to have decided it's us".

Doesn't this realization make Shane look forward
three years and face the fact that if Boyzone do

into the charts
and number ten with our first
single here means our time may be shorter because
we haven't had a year of minor hits to work our way in
slowly," he says.

Shifting his focus to the money that will be made by
Boyzone as a result of their new-found fame Shane
states, quite adamantly, "If there is money to be made
from the band I'm going to make sure I get me share".
So, at the moment, is he happy with the weekly salary
and the way things are going with Walsh and Reynolds?

"It's okay," he says, tentatively. "I can't complain.
But things do change with this hit because all the
money we made in Ireland up to now was going back
into the band. But now we're making more and if
there's serious money to be made in this group,
believe me, I'll be rich. No matter who else is. I'd like
to see the rest of the lads end up with good money,
but I'm going to make sure I do. And if I do make
enough I won't have to go back to a nine-to-five job.
That's my plan. With the hit and the sell-out at the
Point for our gig later this month, it's all going
according to plan."

connections" he made through Boyzone to ensure that his days of employment are not over by the time he reaches 20.

"Having said that, I know Boyzone will work because there is a market for what we're doing in Ireland, that no one else even thought of before. The reaction we get from girls is amazing. At times they really do look like they're going to mob the stage. We are mobbed wherever we go, so we're obviously doing something right!"

Mike Graham is 21 and believes that

Ronan Keating, lead vocalist on *Love Me For A Reason*, was on stage preparing for *Top of the Pops*, while quite sincerely praising the vocal talents of his "rivals" in bands like East 17. Later, looking back he over the past year, he admits that maybe he was right, after all, to leave school to "go for broke" with Boyzone. At only 17, Ronan knows he has to think in the long term and claims if he doesn't get a solo career or go back to acting he intends to "use the even if critics don't take seriously the music being made by Boyzone he has every intention of establishing his credentials as a singer-songwriter.

"I write all my own songs and play guitar and love people like Eric Clapton, Sting and Paul Simon, and 50s and 60s soul classics" he elaborates.

"Ronan and me are writing things for Boyzone so I know that when I get too old for something like this I'm capable as a songwriter and will be trying to make my career out of music in that sense. All my life, music is what I've been aiming for and I know I'm going to make a go of it. I'm fully aware there are people ready to stab me in the back because I'm starting out in Boyzone. But I'm secure in terms of what I'm capable of and, in time, I'll show the begrudgers they were wrong."

When he says "all my life" Mike means it. Like Ronan, he's had the performing bug since he was a child, attending singing, dancing and acting classes long before he joined Boyzone. "That's why I've no problem singing with Boyzone – it's a gig!" he says. "And, it's great to sing for the fans we've made and see that they really do enjoy what we do. Young girls have every right to pick who they want to listen to and, at the moment, thank God, they seem to want to listen to us. I certainly don't feel ashamed to be in Boyzone. And we are out to win. Me and the

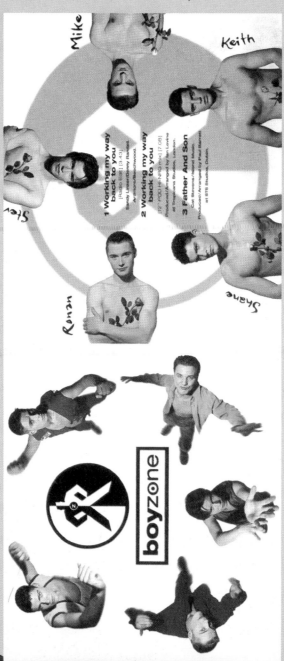

lads will prove what we can do and get recognition in time".

Steve Gately, on the other hand, studied dance for five years, as well as acting and modelling and is a native of Dublin's Seville Place and claims that one of his goals is to put that part of the inner city on the map in a positive way, particularly through becoming famous. However, between rehearsals for *Top of the Pops* he was obviously paying the price of fame, walking round the backstage area of the BBC brandishing a Richard Carpenter autograph he got "for the ma" looking, and obviously feeling homesick. "I am" he says, plaintively. After *Top of the Pops* he rushes back to the rented house in which Boyzone are staying in London, claiming I've had enough of it all for one day, talk to you another time, Joe". One hardly feels like forcing the issue.

Keith Duffy is obviously one of the real hunks in Boyzone and a guy who is clearly streetwise, despite being only 20. A one-time stripper he also wears his sex appeal easily. But what about financially? Isn't the music business riddled with stories of young, handsome guys like Keith being ripped off by unscrupulous managers?

"Although Louis and John are obviously into this for the money they also are legitimate guys so I hope that doesn't happen," he says. "But we're always on the look-out for signs that a record company, or anyone, may be trying to rip us off. That's why the five of us have talks together about all this that no one else hears about, and that includes Louis and John. We all know exactly what we want and know how we're going to go about getting that. And we are determined to stand up for what we feel is due to us. Maybe we should be closer to Louis and John, in this sense, but we're not. Yet we are like five brothers together and will take care of one another that way."

Keith was a student of architecture before joining Boyzone and his father is in the rag trade, therefore taking care of business is second nature to him, he claims.

"I'd hate to go back to architecture but already I've made so many contacts in this business that people say if Boyzone folds I could go into PR or something like that. I'm always thinking along those lines. And let's be honest about this. Boyzone is a pop band not a rock group and a pop band could peak after a year before they disappear. We're not under any illusions about this. We're totally aware of what's going on and that's why we'll fight to get as much out of this as we can, while it's happening."

What about getting as much as they can sexually? How does Keith deal with Boyzone groupies, be they fourteen-year-olds or their mothers?

"Some of them write and say they love you but most do just want to go to bed with you!" he says, smiling. "Even the under-tens write on letters 'bonk me fast, and make it last'; even though they obviously haven't a clue what they're talking about! But what's really interesting is that I was talking to the band Optimistic and they said 'do you know what a fan is?' and I said 'yeah, it's a girl that follows your band' and one of them said 'you're all wrong, fans are girls that

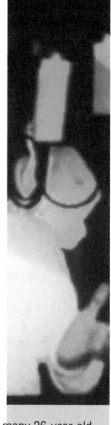

want to sleep with you because you're famous!"

Keith pauses, as if sharing one of pop's great secrets.

"And then he said 'so what you do is flirt and get them more interested in wanting to sleep with you then they'll buy more of your posters, more of your singles and that's what it's all about,'" he says.

Or, you make the decision to sleep with as many as possible, surely?

"That's true, but I've no interest in doing that because some of them are psychos" he says. "On AIDS day they were giving out pieces of cardboard with condoms on them and on the back of the cardboard one fan wrote 'I'll sleep with you, if you'll sleep with me, to Keith, Love, Betty'". She's about 20. I just ignored that the next time I talked to her. Yet when three girls came along I kind of turned away from her for a second and her face was like something out of *Fatal Attraction*. I thought she was going to start a war with these girls. But fans here are different than in Ireland. At home, our fan base ranges from ten to sixteen, over here it's from ten to thirty. We have so

many 26-year-old women following us around, some with mobile phones in their cars telling other fans where we are and what we're doing. Some of them are gorgeous and of the age of consent so God knows what I'd do if circumstances were different. But, at the moment, I wouldn't be into any of that. No matter if you're sleeping around or using protection, if you're male and on the road and bored out of your tits and missing your family and these gorgeous girls come up saying 'sleep with me' it is a temptation".

"Circumstances", in this context, means that previously-mentioned Boyzone management ruling that if they have girlfriends it must be kept a secret. Some of the guys clearly are less than happy with this, and other impositions.

"Part of the imposition is that we have to take care of ourselves, in that we're not supposed to get into fights and aren't allowed to play football in case we hurt ourselves. It's not necessarily that Louis or John really care about us, it's more that they wouldn't want to see the 'merchandise' damaged, which is just how things are," Keith explains, with just a trace of regret, maybe hurt, in his voice.

"And that's the thing about the drugs question," he continues. "We're not allowed do anything that 'might endanger your health' or we'll be out of the band. But, apart from all that, don't get me wrong, despite being tired today and missing people back home we are having the time of our lives doing all this. All we ask is to be left to do the work."

And why, exactly did Keith wave his *Smash Hits* award at the camera and say "everybody back home we made it!"?

"For two reasons," he says. "One was like two fingers to all the critics and begrudgers who put us down and said we'd never do it. So, I was saying 'we *did* bleedin' make it'. And I was saying to me mates and family too,' isn't this great? We did make it.' But, in terms of critics, from being on the *Smash Hits* tour and talking to East 17, EYC and all them pop groups, they told us they get slagged all the time by critics who say: 'So what, you won an award? You're not even a real band.' Hearing that, made us feel a lot better. Because playing clubs around Ireland this year, so often we'd have girls screaming and going crazy but guys'd be spitting and throwing beer bottles at us. That used to get us down. And the thing is, that rock groups don't have to put up with that. We do. So to me, in this sense, us making it is even more of an achievement. And a lot of bands in Ireland who have been slagging us off couldn't break into the British charts to save their lives. But really great bands, like U2 aren't begrudgers and have sent on their congratulations to us and that's what matters. Bill Hughes, who does our videos, said they are behind us a hundred per cent so to hell with the begrudgers! Anyway, in time they'll all have to accept that we are the most successful pop band that came out of Ireland. All we need now is the second hit. Then, I believe, nothing will stop Boyzone."

Tellingly the producers of *Top of the Pops* seem to agree with this analysis. They've already invited Boyzone to appear on the Christmas edition of the show, anticipating that 'Love Me For A Reason' will be at least in the top five by then. They also were deeply impressed by the fact that Boyzone, singing live, got their song in one take during their debut performance on *Top of the Pops*. And, even more tellingly, as we all left the building one producer said "Oh, by the way, I've been asked to tell you that the next time you guys come here you have to provide your own security to deal with all those girls gathering at the gate. We didn't expect that kind of response for a new band on the show.". Obviously, for Boyzone the story has only begun.

CHAPTER 3
THE SECOND SINGLE: THE KEY TO MY LIFE

The Month: February, 1995.
The Date: 21 and 22 February.
The Place: The Old Church, Sandymount, Co. Dublin, where Boyzone are shooting the video for their second single. Outside the railings of the church fans have been gathering since early on the morning of the first day's shooting. Any time there is a break in filming, members of Boyzone wander over to the fans to sign autographs and pose for photos.

Some of the fans, like Celine Weaver, 16, from Irishtown, tell me they "just love Boyzone" because they are "brilliant and beautiful looking." Cathy O' Sullivan, 16, also from Irishtown, puts it more bluntly, saying "Keith is a ride". Debbie Egan, 16, Irishtown cuts across, saying "No, it's Ronan who's massive-looking. Gorgeous!" Paula Egan, 10, on the other hand, just thinks "they're all lovely" and loves them all.

After the video is finally shot I get a chance to sit down and talk with each of the guys at length about how they are responding to success on such an unprecedented scale and ask them to look back and tell me more about how Boyzone really got started, their childhoods, love affairs, families and so on. This, then, is their story, in their words, as they want it told.

Since I first talked to you some would say I have become a heart-throb in Boyzone but, if so, it hasn't gone to my head. I promise! No one around me would allow it to, including me ma and da! They'd kill me if they saw me changing because of this. They say they definitely don't want me to change. And I haven't, as far as they are concerned. when they say that I believe them because I have always been close to my parents, ever since I was a baby. And no one pushed me into this, I choose it myself. I have three brothers and one sister and I'm very close to me sister Michelle. We're all close, especially over the last three years because we've gotten older, but I'm more close to Michelle than any of them. Strangely, none of them had any inclination towards moving into showbusiness, though I did.

"Yet I was good at school, at most everything, especially science and biology and English and art. Like Ronan, I loved English, especially Yeats' poems. I still can say some of them from memory and I think this is one thing that makes Boyzone what we are. We all have those Irish influences, because we are from Ireland and you can't deny that. And we wouldn't want to. That comes across in some tracks on the album, even in terms of the way we count in certain songs! Me ma heard one and said 'Jaysus, that's terribly Irish'. And like a lot of Irish people we love to sing out, from the heart. *Key To My Life* is sung from the heart and a lot of the songs I write come from the heart and are only written down after I work out what they mean, what am I trying to say, exactly. All that comes from the way we study Irish poetry in school. Another track on the new album, *Coming Home Again,* is all about my family, insofar as what I feel when I'm singing it. And that's like a lot of Irish people must feel who have been forced to emigrate. And if I write a ballad I think back on sad times in my life.

"But overall I'd have to say I had a happy childhood, not too much darkness at all. Not that I was spoiled because I was a pretty boy, or anything

like it, at home or at school. I get my downs but they don't last long. Like I was really depressed that day you saw me wandering around the studios of *Top of The Pops* because I wanted to come home. But I'm learning to cope with that, by phoning home a lot. The lads are always giving out because I'm never off the phone! But talking to someone close to me, like me sister, brings a smile to me face and makes me feel good. And they do understand what I have to do so they say 'listen, Stephen, you're going to be alright, so go on back to work, we'll be here when you come home'.

My first serious relationship? I went out with a couple of girls like Siobhan, who was my first. I was 13 and we're still friends. She's pregnant now and having her second child and is really nice. But Siobhan was the first girl I kissed! Then I went out with Anita, then Amanda, then Sharon, then Melissa! But I don't get sexually involved with them. I just get close, as friends, in a cuddly sense. But I think I'll wait a long, long while before I get really involved. I did

love those girls as buddies, no doubt about that. Yet I don't think I've met a person I really, really loved. I loved someone but I don't think it was my biggest love. I could have a bigger love, no problem. If the right person is out there I wish that person would come and get me!

"Yet you really have to put such relationships on hold when you're in a band like Boyzone. If it happens good, if not, that's fine too. My mother always says to me 'the person who is meant for you won't pass you by'. I'm not lonely for a relationship like that, because I really have close friends, like Natalie. She's brilliant and tells me absolutely everything. Same with me. I tell her all my problems, and really trust her. Then there's Sinead, whose another best buddy and we talk about looks, clothes, experiences, sex, everything. A lot of other guys my age only want to talk with women if it means they may get to sleep with them but that's not how it is with me and Natalie and Sinead know that. Natalie has a kid and Sinead is pregnant, so I'm really close to them. And they're both 22 which is something that's always happened in my life, I never had friends the same age as me. The same applies to the girls I went out with as well.

"But because I have so many friends who are girls, I'm extra-sensitive to our fans. You saw me the other day when I went over to sign those autographs in Sandymount. When I'm signing those autographs I never just think 'oh, this is my job and I've got to do it'. I look in their eyes and see that me responding to them as I do is really important to them. You were slagging me for standing back from them but that was only because I was afraid they were going to rob me cap! Usually I go right over to the fans and stand among them. At that day I was looking at the girls and able to tell who really, really wants the autograph. And

the ones who really need to talk to me, or whatever, I will go over to and ask them how they are. And chat. And I did that in Sandymount and the second day we were shooting the video most of the girls I'd singled out came back with teddies for me! And I got a big, huge dolphin off one girl and gave her a big hug and she was delighted, and started to cry. And she had on a hat that said 'Amanda loves Steve'. All that is really important.

"Though, that said, you have to be really careful they don't take that too seriously and then think 'Steve wants me, I know it'. So far I haven't had any

problems along those lines. Though I do get lots of letters, especially dirty ones! I be in bed and me mam gets up early and takes the mail in and reads it. The next thing is that I hear me ma and da breaking their hearts laughing and I go down and say 'so, you'se are at me letters again!' Though if letters are marked 'private' they don't open them! Only the ones that have 'I love you Steve' and hearts and all that on the outside! And the girls who call to the house love me ma. One girl came from county Kerry and she said to me mom, 'Is he there? If he's there and he's sleeping, don't disturb him, I'll be back in half an hour!' and she was gone. But it was belting down rain and when she came back me mom had to tell her I was going on my holidays the next week. But me mom then went and took me favourite, torn jeans and gave them to her! That's how me mam is, though if she's tired she goes to bed and leaves it to someone else to answer the door and deal with the fans. But now they call to talk to her, even when they know I'm not in! All that is great fun. Me mom and dad even have posters of me up in the kitchen! Cheap wallpaper, that's what it is!

"And fans really do care. Like some make me music tapes when I'm going out of the country, saying, 'listen to those when you're depressed'. And they're full of beautiful songs that the fans have really thought about and put in a perfect sequence. It's really sweet of them. And others buy me very expensive presents, like a John Rocha sweater, Calvin Klein underwear and Eternity aftershave, which I love. These are some of the perks of the job, I guess!

"But sometimes it does get very difficult when there are up to fifty fans outside the house and I'm in a hurry somewhere, like here today to do this interview. It's okay if there's only a half dozen and you can talk to them for a while, but with fifty it can get to be too much. And one of the worst experiences I had with the public was in a pub recently when I went in to have a drink and this woman came over and almost dragged me, physically, over to meet some people at her table. I said I'd go over as soon as I relaxed a bit but people can take that as standoffish and attack you for getting 'big-headed', they say. At times like that, I long for the times of solitude I used to know. But I'm not really complaining as fame definitely has its compensations. Like, if I really make money maybe one day I could even buy my own pub! And keep all the troublemakers out!

"But the best part of it all, for me, is performing. Any of the rest of the lads will tell you that whenever I'm on stage I get so much confidence I don't know where it's coming from, I really don't. I get an amazing amount of confidence. On the other hand, when I'm off-stage and standing with loads of girls I'm kinda shy! But on stage I'm brimming with self-confidence and it feels great! Yet the point is that on stage I feel as though I'm in control and I try to look at as many people as possible, just like when I'm signing autographs. I want to make them feel important and to thank them for coming. And it's not that I need the fans to love me. I've got a lot of love in my life, already. But it's nice to know they do love me.

"Yet I'm really not one of those pop stars who craves love and affection from an audience. Let me tell you how much love I get from my family. Every time I leave the house I kiss my mother and tell her I love her and she tells me the same. And she waves at the door to me as I go off down the road. It really gives me a warm feeling. And they're not at all worried about me being in this business. Because of the reasons I told you before, they know I'll never do drugs. And since I talked to you last year the drugs problem in our area has gotten worse. In fact people were happy I highlighted that in the *Irish Times,* and that I said I'd never get into drugs. A couple of people down there have since put together a group trying to do what Boyzone has done. That's great, as far as I'm concerned. Really great. But famous people came, if not from our street, then from our general area, long before me. Like Jim Sheridan, Christy Brown, Luke Kelly.

"I really think Boyzone is going to get even more famous after this next single, *Key to My Life.* Because it really proves th at there is talent in the group.

"We've achieved all our aims in this first year. Our aim last year was to get on *Top of the Pops* and get on the cover of *Smash Hits* and we did that. And that was brilliant and amazing to see. And I, myself, even got

on the cover of *Smash Hits* , which was wonderful, like a thousand dreams come true. I was in the airport coming back from me holidays and I saw my mush on *Smash Hits*. I couldn't believe it! I was in the shop on my own breaking me heart laughing and there were people all around wondering what was wrong with me! I just thought it was so funny!

"Happily, me getting things like the cover of *Smash Hits* doesn't create jealousy among the guys. Because Keith got a cover shot in *My Guy,* and Ronan and Mike got a poster shot, so it all balances out. At the start it created some tension but not now. We all sorted that out and understand that all of this is publicity for Boyzone.

"When I get my share of the money in a month or so what I want to do is buy a house for myself. I may go into property because a lot of people have told us that's a good way to invest. But my own ideal house would be in Dalkey or Killiney, beside Bono! For years I've gone out to Dalkey and Killiney and walked Killiney Hill and sat up there and dreamed of owning my own house up there. And I said 'someday'. But I never knew it would become within my reach so soon! It's now a possibility that I can get a house up there. And as soon as I can I will! Sure, why would you become a pop star if it's not to do things like this with your money? And if I do that, my parents really will be happy for me. Partly because they know I love nothing better than a quiet house, staying in, getting a video, a curry, a couple of cans of beer and that's heaven to me. And it'd really be cute to do that in a lovely house up in Killiney, don't you think?

"Career-wise, what I'd really love to do is act in a feature film, after the Boyzone thing ends. I'd also like to write books. A psychic told me I'd write a book in a couple of years and be successful in that. I already wrote a story when I was in school and that won a prize and was published in a magazine. So, who knows what the future may hold? And the best thing about being in Boyzone and having all these dreams come true is that now I know that other dreams I have could also come true. At this stage I really do believe that anything is possible. Isn't that a gas?"

RONAN

"In childhood, my brother Gary was the one I grew up with. He's five years older than me and he was the closest to me. There's five kids altogether, three brothers and one sister, but when it came to supporting this whole Boyzone thing my folks weren't very happy with the idea at the start. Mostly because, as I told you last time, it meant dropping out of school. And I was the only one at home at the time, because all my other brothers and sister had moved out. Linda, Ger and Garry are living in America. And over the past few years I got very close to Linda, so after the auditions, when I knew I had a place in Boyzone, I gave her a call and asked her what she thought, as mam and dad had said it was my own choice. She said, 'you only live once, Ronan, you may never get an opportunity like this again, so go for it'. And, because of her, I did. And now my folks are behind me big time. It's great. They support me in every way. At the start me mom used to answer the

phone to fans, and take in the mail, but now she understands that she has to get on with her life as well. For a while, Boyzone began to take over her life. Even when she was at work the women'd be asking her 'can you get me Ronan's autograph?' and she'd go crazy. And even now she gets a bit uptight, like this morning, there were half a dozen girls outside my door at half-eight in the morning! And they'll probably be there when I get home.

"But when I told the teachers in school they didn't want me to leave. Even though I was a terrible student, only good at English and maybe art. English was my favourite subject. I loved poetry, particularly Irish poets like Patrick Kavanagh and William Butler Yeats. I really love Yeats and still do a lot of reading of his poetry at home now. It gives me inspiration for writing songs. Apart from Yeats I'm inspired by George Michael and Del Amitri. Their lyrics are incredible. And I'd love to do a duet with George Michael. I also love old albums like *Tea For The Tillerman* by Cat Stevens. That's where I got *Father and Son,* which was the B side on one of our singles. But early on in school my brother, Gar, also influenced my taste in music. He was into A-Ha and I followed them for a while, but later got into my own favourites like Bros. I was a big Bros fan, liked their image, the clothes, the music, everything about them. I used to get a terrible slagging from my mates about that, but I wanted to be up there with the likes of Bros. That was my dream. They put me on the road to all this. But it was the thought of making music that excited me, not the idea of girls screaming, or any of that. Though now that I'm in it, it's a totally different life from what I imagined. Then I thought this would be all glam. I didn't think there'd be so much work involved, on stage, singing, in the studio, doing endless publicity, touring, not eating the right food, not getting enough sleep, having to be nice to everybody and having a contract telling us we can't do certain things that might cause us harm, like go go-carting, ride a motorcycle, do drugs, become an alcoholic and even if we have girlfriends we're not supposed to talk about it. I never knew these were the kind of

impositions put on bands like Bros. But it doesn't undermine fame. I still love it. And I now see that there are rules to this business and if you don't follow them, you don't succeed.

"My first girlfriend? I was very old when I had my first girlfriend, compared to some fellas. I was 13. And when she gave me my first kiss I got the fright of my life! We were at my cousins' party and she was 15, an older woman! But you can imagine what frightened me about that first kiss, though I couldn't say without blushing! All I know is that nothing had ever, let's say, moved me that way! And then I went out with her for about two or three weeks, just to make sure she'd teach me how to kiss like *she* did! And she did! I was 16 when I had my first real date. I brought the girl, whose name I don't remember, to see the film *Cry Freedom* and because I am shy all we did was ask each other, 'Are you alright?', as the film was so sad!

"But I am a romantic, when it comes to girls and this has led to me getting my heart broken. I'm very

sensitive, and soft and the worst heartbreak I ever felt was, last year, when a girl I still know, done something on me and it broke my heart. She went off with another guy and I couldn't believe she'd do that to me. I was in bits and, to this day, it turns my stomach when I think of what she did to me. And it left me feeling very insecure, more insecure than I've always been. As in I'm afraid that any other girl I'd go with will do the same thing on me. I definitely feel that. And she was my first serious girlfriend. Before that it was just casual dates. I didn't know what a relationship was till I met her. It was just messing around with girls before that, one night stands. Though not sexually. I'm still a virgin, the only one left in the band! I choose to be, because I'm waiting for the time to be right. Because I am so romantic about all this the time to make love has to be right or I'm not going to bother. That's just the way I am. And I'm certainly not going to be attracted to someone who's only attracted to me because I'm in Boyzone.

"Like yesterday when you were taking those photographs of us with the fans outside the Church in Sandymount I was listening to them calling us rides and all that and thinking most of them probably don't even know what the word means! I do take all that kind of stuff with a pinch of salt. I'm very careful not to offend the fans, especially when they're hands are reaching out, with their little autograph books, but you can only give them so much. If you give too much it gets to you and it gets to them. You have to step back. Like when they're screaming for a kiss or saying 'Ronan, do you remember me from...' wherever. You say, 'yeah' but often you don't remember and it's no use troubling yourself because you can't remember them all. But they all want you to remember and can be hurt if you don't recognize them because they've built up this special relationship with you in their minds. Yet the danger is that if you do show that you remember them they can think you're really into them and become obsessive. If you even remember their names they think they are your friends and then complain that you don't give them enough time and say, 'so, what's happening to you? Are you getting big-headed?' They don't understand this is just our job and what we do. So you have to be very careful when it comes to the fans. And a lot of them, when they

write 'I love you' on letters, make you realize they probably don't even know what love is. Especially the very young ones. All they're really saying is, 'show me I exist, tell me I'm your most important fan', and it's sad, really.

"The highlight of our first year, for me, was coming back and accepting the Entertainment Award here in Dublin. That was like two fingers to everybody who'd put us down! When we finished that number in the Concert Hall and got one of the loudest claps of the night the hair stood up on the back of my neck! It was incredible!

"When we started off we got so much grief from people in Ireland, in particular, because we were 'just a pop band' or supposed to be taking off Take That. But getting to number one in the Irish charts did shut so many of those begrudgers up and gave us the last laugh. It was the same when we went to the top of the British charts. And writing *Key To My Life* and having it as our next single is going to shut up even more of our detractors because it shows we're not just a cover band doing songs that were originally hits for other people. Me, Mike and Steve wrote it.

"Even if it's not a hit the point is that it's a song we wrote ourselves and it shows we can do it. But we all know it's going to be a hit! And if it is, hopefully, we'll never have to bring out another cover version. Or, maybe only occasionally.

"We've got a big publishing deal coming up soon, which means we'll get a huge advance for all the songs we're going to write. That will be split between the five of us and make us all quite rich little more than a year after forming the band. But the money has to be split five ways, otherwise we'd kill each other, as money can be the root of all tension. It definitely can be when it comes to the music business and someone decides that the people who write songs should get a bigger share than the people who just sing them. That's happened to us, but at least the advance will be split between us all and the rest will be broken down according to who earns what. But if I write the songs I'm going to make sure I get the money. The same applies to Mike and whoever.

"I don't think that finally getting this huge amount of money will make me less hungry in terms of fame and riches. In fact, I think it'll make me more hungry! I'm not going to say I'm not in Boyzone for the money, of course I am! But not one hundred per cent just for the money as I do also love music and I love performing and entertaining people and writing songs. But I do want to make money out of all this, especially from recording my own songs and maybe having other people record our songs. Like, we made a whole lot of money for Donny Osmond when we recorded his song *Love Me For A Reason*!

"I'm reading George Michael's biography, *Bare*, at the moment and that's really opened my eyes to the way the music business operates and can screw people financially. If I'd read this before going into the music business I probably wouldn't have joined

Boyzone, or believed all that kind of wheeling and dealing can happen. It's so sad that he's not going to record another track until after the year 2000. The world shouldn't be without another George Michael song. George Michael is an inspiration for me on another level as he is one of the few teen idols, along with maybe Michael Jackson, to make the transition into adult stardom. So it's terrible that his career was hijacked by music business shenanigans. But what reading his book has done is made me realize that if there is money to be made from this band we're going to make it ourselves. And as soon as I can afford it I'm going to buy a house! But not for myself. I'll rent it out! I definitely don't want to go splashing my money about on cars and all the things you're supposed to buy when you become a pop star. In fact, I'd like to buy a garage for my brother, who's a mechanic. And I'd like too buy a restaurant for my sister, who has a restaurant in New York. Gerard works in the stock exchange in New York so he's alright, financially. In fact, he advises me about investments and stocks and shares and all that. But, more than all this, I'd buy my folks a house in the country. They love the country and hate Dublin. My father's from Cavan and mother's from Raheny, in Dublin and maybe it's not so much that they hate Dublin but they want to live in the country and if I can help them do that, to repay them for all they've done for me, then I will. And, as for myself, I'd like to live in Clontarf, in County Dublin, which is a good investment as well! All that would, of course, be part of preparing to get married and settling down. I don't want to be judged on Boyzone as if that alone defines who I am. There's far more to me than being a member of Boyzone. And already I've found it's hard to take anyone seriously as your real friend if all they're attracted to is you being a member of a pop band. To tell you the truth, since I became famous I've never had so many wannabe friends in my life. All that makes me very suspicious and cynical. I must admit that I don't particularly enjoy the fact that I can no longer walk the streets of Dublin without getting mobbed. I can't go into the city centre anymore, even to do some shopping. And I miss that, because I grew up in ways in Dublin city centre, as a result of working for four years in a shoe store in my spare time. I grew up very quickly because of that, too quickly, because I started going into pubs before I should have gone into them, and so on. Sometimes I wish I'd never have done that, at fourteen, whatever, that I'd remained climbing trees, cycling my bike, throwing stones, or whatever. Especially now that I'm also having to grow up extra fast, at 17, because I'm a member of Boyzone. In that sense I kind of lost my childhood, and adolescence twice. But then, that's a feeling I often work into my songs, which is turning something negative into something positive. Myself and Steve wrote a song on this theme, which is very important to us, called *Coming Home Now*. And that's written because we travel so much and now have to spend so much time out of Ireland. Because of that we do long to get home and always are reminded that Dublin is the best city in the world. It really is so good to land in Dublin airport and look over to the left and see them Ballymun flats. You know what I mean? Isn't it? That's what we all were aching for that day you were with us at *Top of the Pops*. And it then was so good to come home for Christmas. And *Coming Home Now* says everything we feel about this whole subject. It's on the new album and we all sing on it, which is also very important to us. The best thing about the new album is that 75% of the songs are our own originals.

"But whether the new album and new single are hits or not we always try to remember that teenage fans do forget very quickly. Bros were there one day then gone the next. And Boyzone never forgets that. Or, even in terms of Take That. Their new single shows that they see the writing on the wall and are trying to get the older audience now. But we don't see Take That as our rivals. We like the guys and think there is enough room there for all of us. And we're quite aware that in another two, three, five years another group could come along to replace us. Maybe Babyzone!"

"As you can see from the childhood photos I gave you for this book, I do come from a very close family. We've always been close and because we're all a musical family they're all behind me in terms of Boyzone. And when it comes to the critics who have been saying we don't even write our own songs I can't wait to see them eat their words when they hear the new single or the seven songs on the album we have written ourselves. In fact I'm the type of person who, when someone is putting them down, will fight his damnedest to prove those people wrong. One thing I can't take is people from the streets criticizing us because we made it. Let's face it, there are a lot of bums out there who don't want to better themselves. I do, so I'm not going to let that criticism get to me. This is my job, I do it well and I get paid good money for doing it and if anyone doesn't like that they can go to hell.

"What I'm going to do with my money is buy property. As thick and naive as some people might think we are, as far as finance is concerned we're totally on top of the case and have already learned a lot in this business about how to make money and keep it. There are a lot of sharks out there in the music business and that's one fact we've woken up to this year. No sharks are going to get Boyzone.

"I'll hold onto my publishing royalties, for example, and hopefully somebody will record my songs and make millions for me. That's the way the business works. *Key To My Life* could be covered. Another I composed the words and music for, *You*, I am really proud of. It's a song aimed at someone you're in love with, telling her how she's made you feel and how she's changed your life. It's a very personal song to me.

"Looking back on my first girlfriends I sometimes think there's probably a few who would now wish they'd stayed with me. Some have given me a call to congratulate me but then, later on, they give you another call, saying 'fancy going for a drink?' but I see through that and say, 'no, thanks, anyway'.

"But I must admit that I've broken one or two hearts in my time. And my heart has been ripped apart. Absolutely. There was one stage around the age of 19 when a relationship ended very badly and left me delving into myself wondering why it had finished, and about life in general. A lot of teenage lads go through that kind of thing at 19, as you move through that change between your imagining of life and actually meeting its hard realities.

"What hurt me about that relationship is that love had turned from something that was sweet, sexy, romantic to something dark and painful. How something like that could happen overnight, and someone could just change, really tore me up. And that's what happened. We'd been seeing each other for a couple of months but then, after one night, I was just dropped. I did write a few songs about it but

when I look at them now I realise I'm past that state, and those lyrics are so dark they couldn't be used for a Boyzone album. Maybe after Boyzone, if I go on as a solo artist I'll release one or two. And I probably should because we all know that when you're feeling down and blue the thing you do is listen to sad songs, things you can relate to and find comfort in. I certainly do. But then I guess even *Love Me For A Reason* could be a cry from the heart for some of our fans.

That relationship, at 19, was my first serious relationship. As far as my first kiss is concerned. I was 8 and she was 10 and she was from London and was a cousin of a neighbour of mine. So I was her boyfriend and we were playing one day and she kissed me and used her tongue and I didn't like it at all! I thought it was horrible! After that I was frightened to kiss her, to say the least. And I'm still not mad about the tongue. That turned me off a bit!

"In terms of sex some of the fans really turn me off at times too. Like the other day one 12-year-old girl said 'Mike, I'd do anything for you, if you know what I mean' and I just felt it was sad. And even those twenty-something fans you've heard about, who follow us in their cars, the closest they'll ever get to us is a hotel lobby. Like we do sit down and have a drink with them, but then it's goodbye, no matter what they may be offering or what's on their minds. We just go up to bed, lights out and asleep, and because we usually have an early start there's no time for messing. A lot of people would assume we take girls up from the lobby to our rooms but I swear to you, we don't. Besides, you never know who you're bringing to your room. It could be a headcase, who could knife

just too dangerous. So I just say goodnight and goodbye.

Because I grew up in the age of AIDS it is something I'm always aware of. It is something you have to be very careful of, and make sure you practice safe sex. Anyone who doesn't really is being silly and irresponsible. In terms of using condoms and all I don't think enough is done about all this in Ireland. It's stupid the way the government has responded to AIDS. They don't realise there are kids out there starting to have sex at 13, 14 and they haven't a clue about safe sex. I hope those fans of ours who are saying they'd do anything for us sexually, are taking care when they have sex with someone else. But I really don't think they're getting the proper sex education in Ireland, whatever about England and other countries abroad. Even guys of my generation, though they're aware of the dangers, probably just go for it if they get a chance to have sex with some girl, and don't even think of safe sex. So, in ways it's up to the girls to make sure a fella wears a condom.

you in the back. Anyway, none of us have any interest in bringing girls back to our rooms, for whatever reasons, And even if it is because we have girlfriends I can't tell you because we're supposed to at least say we're young, available and single. That's part of the whole thing and I go along with that. Besides you don't know these women and in the age of AIDS it's

"Ireland is the same in terms of educating people against the dangers of drink and drugs. It's useless. When I was in school we done sex education in primary school – but only twice. At 22 I'm still finding out things about sex that I should have known years ago. Same with school in relation to drink and drugs where we got even less education. I don't remember ever sitting down for a specific lesson about drugs. It was just maybe a five-minute topic that arose in some class, or whatever. And that, too, is silly, when you think that we now are in the 'E' generation. I've never taken 'E' and wouldn't want to and the reason why is because I'd be afraid to. Especially now that we're learning it does damage the brain. I don't like not being in control of myself. I don't drink because I'm not into the buzz drink gives. I'll take a drink occasionally but, overall, I'm not into it. I'm not a preacher, people can do what they want but I'm out to look after myself and part of that is not to get hooked on drink or drugs, especially now that I'm part of the music business where so many people you meet are into drugs or drink. If someone in the music business trues to force drugs on me I'll break their face. I just don't want anything to do with drugs.

"Apart from that, I'm really angry at the Irish school system because there are so many people suffering due to the lack of sex education, and drink and drug abuse advice in Irish schools. It's a disgrace.

"These are the kind of subjects I'd write about in songs if, in any way, I could help keep a kid away from such things. If they're feeling they could turn towards drugs I'd love to write, or say, or sing something that might make them turn away. Boyzone did a photo-call in a Dublin school to help publicize an anti-drugs seminar. I'm happy to get involved in anything like that. In fact, to me that's one of the perks of becoming famous. That people do ask you to support worthwhile things like anti-drug crusades. I hate to see kids my age either thinking about or getting into the drugs scene at 20. To be realistic about it, their lives could end very soon, after – what – 20 odd years in the world when they could have lived to be 80? It's a terrible waste. I understand why someone of 20, who is unemployed, doesn't want to look ahead to another 60 years in such circumstances but drugs aren't the answer.

"I felt really, really low at one stage. I had my family and friends around me but no one could really understand what I felt, after that girl ditched me and other things seemed to push me into a major down phase. Now, at that time, I wanted to escape from the depression but not through drugs or drink. And I'm glad I didn't. Because look what was around the corner for me – Boyzone. So it really is better if people hold on. Drugs won't solve your problem. Because, like, when you are drinking, the problem is still there after the drink wears off. So, what's the point, really? You have to face your problem and sort it out without drink and drugs. Then go out and get drunk to celebrate, which is a different thing!

"Let's face it, we're not doing Ireland any favours by pushing this drunken Irishman image. We're a new generation and it's time we showed the world that the Irish are not like that now. The same applies to Boyzone being a band from the northside of Dublin. We're not The Commitments and, in fact, one thing we encounter all over Europe is amazement when people see that Ireland can produce a clean-cut pop band like Boyzone, especially those people who thought that all young Irish people now are like the Commitments. We're not. And that's why I think so many people seem to want to help us. It's weird but people actually like us in the music business. Because we are young and fresh and because we're Irish. Being Irish, in particular, is really trendy these days. Everywhere we go they seem to love us. Especially people in places like Italy who, until now, only saw Ireland in terms of U2 or the troubles in Northern Ireland. Same in Belgium and the Netherlands. In those places, maybe they're also aware of our traditional music but not our pop scene.

"The best thing about those countries is that pop rules their charts not rock. So Boyzone fits in really neatly with what is in their charts and the kind of stuff they prefer. It's great for us. Because, unlike Ireland, here is no snobbery at all when it comes to pop band like us. That's one thing I don't like about the Irish. There are so many begrudgers in this country trying to bring down anyone who gets ahead. It's hard enough to make something of yourself in this country, where there is so much unemployment, so you'd think they'd give you a clap on the back when you make it abroad, as we have.

"That said, what I've realized is that if you can please an Irish audience you can please anybody. So if we're this big here we might even make it in America, which is a dream we all have. In fact, after we have a few hit singles in Ireland and England and Europe the next step for Boyzone must be to conquer America.

"Either way, my ultimate aim for Boyzone is that we get five, ten years out of this, though we all know it could be over tomorrow. we certainly won't be doing a kind of Manzone at fifty years of age, that's obvious! But after Boyzone I'd like to carry on as a solo artist, having attained some kind of credibility in this band. In fact, I'd like to do what Sting did after he left Police. I'd love to follow in his footsteps. That's my ultimate dream.

"On a personal level I just want peace of mind and, one day, marriage and children. But when that happens I'll probably buy a house and move out of the city because I feel that, at heart, I'm just a country boy! That's where I get peace, in Kerry, Dingle, wherever. I was in Dingle a few weeks ago and there's really nothing like it on earth. So, a dream would be to get a house there or somewhere like Greystones in County Wicklow. And, with the luck of God I will be able to buy such a house soon. And I do thank God for all this. I know it's not trendy, or anything, but I do believe in God and I know that I must take full, and good advantage of this gift he's given me. He gave it to me and he could take it away just as quickly. This conversation comes up a lot in private conversations between us lads in Boyzone. I'm not sure we all agree on the same thing but we definitely know that what we've been given is a gift and we mustn't abuse it. As I said to you before, I also believe I was born to do this and I was just waiting for the chance. Now I have it and I'm not going to screw things up. I have my faith in God and believe in God and owe it to him to make sure this turns out right for me, and for all of us. At least, as much as I can. I'm not ashamed to admit to that faith in God. Without him I really believe I wouldn't be in Boyzone. It really is one of the best things that's ever happened in my life."

SHANE

"I was always a very active child, I done a lot of sport in school and on weekends I used to go to gymnastics, which I started at about ten. Before that I done a lot of swimming and used to win a lot of the races, though I don't actually know if I was doing that to try and make something of myself, or not. But I was always good at sport, though I hate football!

"I have no brothers, five sisters and I'm kind of close to them, some more than others. I probably would have liked a little brother to take care of, but I never felt the need for a big brother to look after me. How my sisters influenced me is that their tastes in music pushed me in the direction of why I wanted to be a pop star. They now love Boyzone but they used to listen to Bros and New Kids on the Block and I used to think 'God, I want to be like that'.

"The first record I remember hearing was at my older sister, Tara's party. Someone gave her a New Kids on the Block tape for her birthday and I played that all the time. I really loved them from the beginning, though the first record I ever bought was an NWA record, which I loved because of the way rappers talk about the ghetto and the bad language they use! I still listen mostly to rap, like Ice Cube and, because of that, can see how some kids who love rap or hip-hop think Boyzone are wimps. But then, at one stage, all I wanted to hear was music about guns and gangsters and I used to slag off all the boy bands saying they were just for the girls! It was more that they were for my sisters, not me. But now I love the

songs we do as much as I love rap, though I realize they are worlds apart. In fact, I like singing ballads more than anything because they help me express things I find hard to put into words in other ways. To sing a ballad and think of a girl you lost can nearly make you cry. So now I love rap to play in a car and our music for other situations, though we have done dance tracks and I love them.

"But to go back to the beginning, I was a kid and New Kids on the Block originally fired this dream to become a star, I guess. The main reason I wanted it, of course, is that all the girls are into that and any normal young lad would want girls to look at him the same way and go 'isn't he brilliant?'.

"And I did need that, because I wasn't that confident at 13, 14, though people said I was a good-looking kid. In fact, I don't think I ever, in my life approached a girl. I was always too shy for that, because though I knew I was pretty my ego would have been shattered if I was rejected or refused if I asked a girl out. I never had the confidence to do that. Especially if it was someone I really wanted to be with, and get close to.

"My first girlfriend, if you can call her that, was a girl I met in low babies and I had a smock on to do painting with and I was bawling my eyes out because I didn't want to wear a smock! She came over and was saying 'it's okay' and I remember, not kissing her, but being with her a lot and becoming quite good friends. I would have been 6 or 7 at the time and her name was Debbie Hughes. We never dated but we were close for about three years. My first serious relationship was the one I was in before I joined Boyzone. It lasted until after I was in the band but, y'know, we're not allowed to have a girlfriend in this. And I do

guess. And you do get romantic letters along those lines from girls who just want to hug you, apart from the ones who say they want to jump all over your bones!

"But I do miss having a girlfriend sometimes, Often when I go home and talk to my mates and they say 'we were out in Tamangos night-club and such-and-such was with that girl from years ago' I think 'I'd love to have been there'. But then I tell them about a trip to Austria, as part of Boyzone, so this does have its compensations! It works both ways, really. But I don't go on about Boyzone with me mates. I tell them what I've done, end of story. Then we talk about cars, the usual stuff, and I'm just Shane as they know me not Shane from a pop band.

"Yet you do lose out in certain ways. Like I can't play certain sports because I'd be afraid of even twisting my ankle and not being able to do a gig. And when I go into pubs now I do be quite afraid of some jealous guy maybe slashing a bottle in my face because he wants to ruin my looks, or whatever. I've had people try to start trouble along those lines but I usually walk away. It certainly happened a lot when the first single came out in Ireland. But now 99 per cent of guys come over and say 'fair play to youse'. Now it's more jealous girls, or girls who are into rock not pop who come up and say 'you faggots, do you call that music?' That's another reason for wanting to have a girlfriend! Because when you don't have one people say you are gay.

"We came home from Rome the other night and Mike got out of a taxi and there was this girl and fella sitting on a pillar with their arms around each other and the girl shouts over 'you faggot' and I had to laugh at that! That's so Irish. If they can't tear you down one way they'll tear you down another way!

"But when I stop and think about the kind of girl I'll probably end up with I'd have to say she'll probably be someone who says 'no' the first time I ask her to go on a date! If she said no, I'd chase her because I'd know she has no interest in me being in Boyzone and all that nonsense. So then if I get to know her and she

still love her, I guess. But then if I don't have a girlfriend I can concentrate more on my career and on being nice to fans. If I had a girlfriend I might be standoffish with fans because I'm afraid she'd get jealous, or whatever. And if she was ever at a concert I wouldn't play to a crowd half as much, because I'd be afraid of her saying, 'would you look at him, acting up for all the other women!' So having a girlfriend might hurt my performance because I wouldn't like to hurt her by being seen singing to other girls, basically. My whole job is to sing to girls and make them want me so having a girlfriend would be too much hassle. The kind of girl I like is someone who is not too loud, someone shy. A girl who doesn't think she's God's gift to men and isn't always checking out guys to see if they're looking at her. I also like small girls, I can't stand tall girls! I love a small girl who comes up to my chest and who I can hug and make feel protected, I likes me for me then we'll probably get together. But if I met a girl and she said 'I'd love to go out with you, because I love Boyzone' I'd probably go on that one date then end of story. Too many girls out here just want the picture, the guy on stage, the fella who sings the song. They don't know who I am. They don't know if I'm a jerk or the soundest bloke on earth. All they know is that I'm an attractive fella and I'm famous and that's all they need to know, it seems. They just want a bit of me because I'm famous and that's not enough, as far as I'm concerned. But if I do get into a relationship before Boyzone ends I'll keep it quiet and take it as it comes.

"When I look back at my schooldays the one thing I remember is that I was actually asked to leave school because I didn't actually do anything! I'd no interest in school, whatsoever. I'd come in, sit down, but wouldn't even bring me books and wouldn't listen. I hated school, all I wanted to do was go out and drive a motor bike or a car. I remember once I was in an English class and everyone was talking, except me, because I was so bored. The English teacher gave us homework, saying we had to write it out three times and I said out loud 'oh, for God's sake!' and she threw me out of the class. Then I was sent to the Principal's office and he said, 'all you do is pose around this school, you're a waste of space and basically I could have a student that wants to work in here, so I really don't think you should come back next term'. And I was happy with that. But I didn't tell my parents that and still haven't. They'll read it in this book! At the time I told them it wasn't a good education I was receiving and that I'd rather leave school and become a mechanic and that's what I did. Anyway, in third year, I'd done a lot of mitching from classes because I just didn't want to be in school at all. So I was glad to get out. And I'm still glad I left, or was thrown out!

At the time there also was a hard time in my family, hassle to do with one of my sisters, and I wasn't in the mood for going to school. I was very upset about it all. So I used to get on my motorbike and go down to the beach and stay there for the day.

That was when I was 14, 15. But by the time I was 17 I was a mechanic, driving a car and happy as I could be before I went into the pop business.

"When Boyzone ends, I'll get out of the music business because I don't have enough confidence to go solo. I also don't think I'd enjoy it. Us five lads when we're together even help each other through the hard times of being lonely. I don't think I could handle that on my own. So I reckon if I make my money, have good memories, enjoy my life up to the age of 22, or whenever it's going to end, I'll be happy with that. And what I'll do is invest in property and live off that. In that sense I know exactly what I'm doing and where I'm going.

"Yet when I do look back, I'll always remember things like the audition for Boyzone. I knew the first day the auditions were held that I had the gig. Because myself and another guy went to Louis Walsh to ask him about forming a pop band. Louis liked our attitude and we gave him the idea for Boyzone and he set up the auditions, so I knew I was in from the start. But when I saw all the people at the auditions I was taken aback by the experience of all those other guys. Some of them had sung in bands, whereas I hadn't, though I did sing in a few choirs. Then I started to worry and wonder, 'should I really be here?' And on the very last day of auditions there was ten people in the room and I was one of them and I still didn't know if I had the right to be there, because I still hadn't developed much confidence – though I have now! On the last day I was really afraid my name wasn't going to be called out, but it was and I felt blessed. And I still feel blessed to be part of Boyzone. That was real relief, to hear them call my name. I just said to myself 'thank God!'

"The real highlight for me was wining the *Smash Hits* award. Being on telly was a highlight at the start but not our first *Late, Late Show*, where we were so bad it was embarrassing! But then we didn't even know each other's names at that point! And on the night I was thinking when we danced, 'this has killed us before we even get started!' But it didn't. And now if I saw that clip on video I'd get such a laugh because there is such a distance between that and us on the *Smash Hits* show.

"That show was a highlight for me because I remember when the band first started, sitting at home in my room alone and looking at the *Smash Hits* show

thinking 'imagine if that was us next year!' And then when we got there and won that award it was unbelievable! But if it could happen for us that fast we also know it can end that fast. So we're going to make the best of it while we can. Yet I do get dizzy sometimes, like realizing that *Love Me For A Reason* is in the charts in eight countries right now and we're not even together a year and a half! That's what amazes us all most of all. We've already gotten to a point, in terms of success, that takes other bands years to achieve. So, in ways we know that everything is possible for us. But one thing I'd love to do before Boyzone breaks up is prove everyone wrong who, from the start mocked us by saying 'Boyzone, they're crap and they'll never do anything. They're going nowhere'. And to meself I want to prove that a normal Joe Soap who was a mechanic can do something with his life. I want to be able to turn around to me own kids one day and say 'your dad was a mechanic and look what he became just by being in the right place at the right time'".

KEITH

I was dancing in the P.O.D when Louis asked if he could talk to me, brought me into the VIP lounge and asked if I'd like to be in a pop band. That's how it all got started for me. But, by coincidence, at that stage there was already a picture in the paper of the other two guys who were going to be in a pop group and I'd thought, 'what have they got that I haven't got? They're going to make a fortune and I'd love to get involved in that'. I had met Shane in the gym three weeks before Louis Walsh approached me so I knew all about the band before he even asked. So I said, 'are we going to make loads of money?' and he said 'yeah'. So I said, 'then I'll have a piece of that!' So he told me to come along to the final audition and I did my bit there and got the gig! And I wasn't confident at all, especially about singing as I'm not one of the strongest singers in the band and they'd be the first to tell you that!

But I can hold a note and I know I'm not ugly so, in ways, that's enough to be at least one of the members of a band like Boyzone. The song I did in my audition was *Piano Man* by Billy Joel because me father used to sing it and I know all the words. Then they played *I'm Too Sexy For My Shirt* and asked me to do a routine dance to that, which was no problem to me because two weeks before that I'd done a strip-o-gram to the same song! So I did my strip in the audition, though I only took off my waistcoat and shirt! But I think that's what got me the gig! Though we did have to do one more audition and I sang *You've Lost That Lovin' Feeling* by the Righteous Brothers because I sing that a lot when I'm drunk! So that's how it all got started for me, in Boyzone. And the next night after we were told we were in the band Louis put us on the *Late, Late Show*! And I'm thinking 'we're stars already' but, as Shane said to you, we were a disgrace that night!

"I was thinking of that when we did the National Entertainment Awards from the National Concert Hall. I think we gave our best performance that night. I've watched Take That and East 17 but that night we were as sharp as a knife and that's when I really knew we had it made.

"One thing that's changed since you and me first talked last year is that I don't get to see the mates I was telling you about then and I miss that. I just don't have the time to meet up with them as much as I used to, or would like to. In that sense, Boyzone has taken over my life. I've one close friend and I got to see him recently and I phone the others but Keith, Owen, Paul, Gav and meself don't get together like we used to. When we do get together we're as close as we ever were and I hope that never changes. We never were the kind of macho idiot gang guys can be when they get together. We say the right things when things need to be said. Like, at Christmas, we said 'I love you, man, you're a great mate and in a couple of years we'll be bringing our kids down St. Stephen's Green together, right?' we're not afraid to be soppy with each other and that's what's great about us.

"Though in Ireland, in particular, Boyzone do get a lot of flak about being queers. In London we do have a gay following and one guy bought us all bottles of after-shave for Christmas that cost forty pounds a bottle. So fair play to him! But we were here in Dublin doing *Surprise, Surprise* with Cilla Black here last week and a guy went by and shouted, 'you're just a shower of queers' but that doesn't bother me. He was probably jealous. What gets me is why don't they praise us for making it, not slag us. Because, first you had the likes of Take That now Ireland has shown it can produce its own band along those lines.

Until now you had such bands coming to Ireland, selling out the Point Depot two nights in a row and taking all that money out of Ireland whereas now we do it and the money stays here. And we are Irish, which is something everyone should be proud of, surely?

"And, let's face it, Boyzone are something different for Ireland. Sure we have thousands of rock bands but they're all the same, basically. I'm not putting rock down as I've always been into rock bands like Bon Jovi and U2 and Metallica. Because of that, to be quite honest with you, if I wasn't in Boyzone I wouldn't have even listened to a song like our first single, *Working My Way Back To You*. I didn't like it at all and wouldn't have bought it. But *Love Me For A Reason* is a cool song and people listen to it in clubs and slow-dance to it, which is great. So, to me our music is legit. Having said that, though our new single, *Key To My Life* is, again, a good ballad, I wouldn't buy it! But I would buy the dance mix of it! It's brilliant. And *Coming Home* is another great song on the album. And, despite all the rock bands in Ireland who slag us, the biggest band thinks we're okay! U2 have congratulated us and wished us the best of luck and that means a lot to us. They were very friendly when we met them. And while guys like Take That are also friendly to us, they are worried because so many people are saying we're the first pop band to come along in years who are contenders for their crown. The other contenders are East 17 but they're more of a macho band than a pop group. Bad Boys Inc aren't going to go much further than they've gone so we really could make it all the way. But I'm no fool. I know that the people who buy our records and have made us successful are mostly young fans who like nice songs, sweet tunes and good-looking fellas in a band. That's what sells, so that's what we're doing! Just like rock bands do what they know will sell. At that level we're all at the same thing.

"The fans are great fun, like that girl yesterday who shouted at me 'Keith, if you're a virgin, I'd love to break you in!' I got a Valentine's card last week which my mother saw, not me, and in it was knickers and bra! Me ma threw them out and the letter was all about what that girl would and wouldn't do to me in bed! A lot of them would drop dead if you wrote back and said, 'oh yeah? Come on then!' It's easy for them to deal with the fantasy, but not facts. And maybe it's good for them to write those letters, to get things off their chests! But you have to be careful how you respond to such letters because if you turn one fan against you, by rejecting her, she could turn hundreds against you just by word-of-mouth.

"Like Shane, I prefer girls who are smaller than me. And with blond hair and green eyes. I've a fascination with green eyes, believe me! I think they're amazing! And I like a nice pair of legs and boobs! But in terms of characters I like someone who is outgoing and not afraid to make a show of herself if she's with me. Because when I'm away from the band I just go wild, and I like a girl who likes to go wild with me!

From meeting all the other pop groups we know what's going on and we know a lot of them do drugs. We don't. None of us do. It's not just that it says we can't do drugs, as part of our contract. If I wanted to do drugs, I would. But we don't do drugs because we don't want to. In my contract it says they can suspend me if I do drugs but they're not going to suspend me because it's my face people want to see. But I wouldn't do drugs, because I don't want to and I wouldn't want to ruin Boyzone for the others.

"One thing I didn't tell you last time about that architecture course I was doing is that I used to get a lot of attention from the girls in the college and I'm sure that made the guy who was teaching me jealous, as he was only a couple of years older and he was quite good-looking himself. I did get into a lot of trouble with him.

In terms of women, I was photographed with some girls on me holidays in the *News of the World* and that upset some fans so we have to keep what we're doing private. The fans don't like to think you have a girlfriend. And I understand that, though I didn't at first. It doesn't matter if they never kiss you or are never with you, as long as they know you're single they think they have a

chance. But if the older girls in particular find you are going out with someone they get very annoyed.

"In Ireland our fans are very young but in other countries they are mature 20-24-year-olds, and

older.They're the ones with the mobile phones and cars and they follow us everywhere.They really get angry if they see you with a girl and you're not supposed to have any girlfriend.

"Yet I remember the first girl I kissed. I was 11 years of age and I was in fifth year and this girl I was going out with was in sixth year. She was 12. We were going out with each other and hadn't even kissed. One night we were baby-sitting and we were on the couch and I hadn't a clue what to do, though I knew you were supposed to open your mouth or something! So she said 'no tongues' and I was like a goldfish kissing her and thought I was great! But I had one eye on the streetlights because I knew once they came on I had to race home. So I ran out, and home, and dashed through the kitchen and was terrified my dad was going to know I'd been kissing a girl! So I splashed cold water all over me lips, in case me dad could see what I was doing. But I've stopped doing that now, when I kiss girls!

"Yet although I'm a real romantic I'm sometimes to blame for getting my own heart broken. Like there was one girl I was going out but I was dating other girls at the time and, feeling guilty, I told her and only later realized I loved her. But we all make mistakes in love, don't we?

"The great thing is that little more than a year after me saying to Louis, 'is there money to be made from this?', I'll get big money as part of the record deal advance we're getting soon. At the moment all we get paid for are gigs, but in a few months the money will be rolling in from all angles. Yet even though, at the start, I admit I went into this for money, once you get a taste of fame you don't really just do it for the cash. You do it for the sole enjoyment of it.

"The sole enjoyment, for me, is that you never forget what your priorities are. You can go along with all these interviews, photo sessions, videos, live shows, radio, television all over the world and just get depressed because you forget what you're doing it for. But then comes the moment you walk out on stage, see the crowd, hear them scream and you say, 'this is what it's all about'. Nothing on earth compares to that experience. And no amount of money can buy that feeling. It's really what I live for now. To walk onto a stage and see 6,000 people screaming for you is the biggest thrill of all, no matter how much hard work you have to do to get there. You saw the two days we put into just making the video for *Key To My Life*. It was hard work. But the thrill from performing on stage compensates and leaves an awful lot to spare, believe me. I could easily get addicted to that feeling, let me tell you! I can't wait to perform on stage again.

"What I'm most looking forward to is us having four, five hit albums and the same amount of number ones before I leave this band. That would be ideal, as far as I'm concerned. Plus, to be secure financially because of it all, so I can look back and say 'I don't regret a moment with Boyzone'. I could make enough to be financially secure for the rest of my life. Take That have been going for five years and they are financially secure for the rest of their lives. So it can be done. They're all millionaires. Put a million pounds in the bank and you could live off the interest alone for the rest of your days. That's the ultimate aim I have. And we'll easily do that if we do a world tour and, especially, if we make it in America. If we make it in America we have it made for life. That's really a dream. I'd love to break America.

I'd love to get huge in South Africa, but for more of a personal reason. I have an uncle who used to live with us and he's like a brother to me. He got into a lot of trouble when he was 16 and he done a runner to South Africa. His mother and father came home when he was 18 and he stayed over there. Yet I haven't heard from him in a long time, though I believe he's after getting married and has kids. He married a black girl and she's the daughter of a king in South Africa. So I'd love to get famous over there so he could point me out as his nephew and be proud of me. That'd really be important to me. Maybe even more important than making it in America, which I think we will anyway. As you yourself said in *Hot Press* 'the Boyzone story has only just begun'!

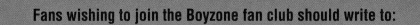
Fans wishing to join the Boyzone fan club should write to:

PO Box 102
Stanmore
Middlesex
HA7 2PY

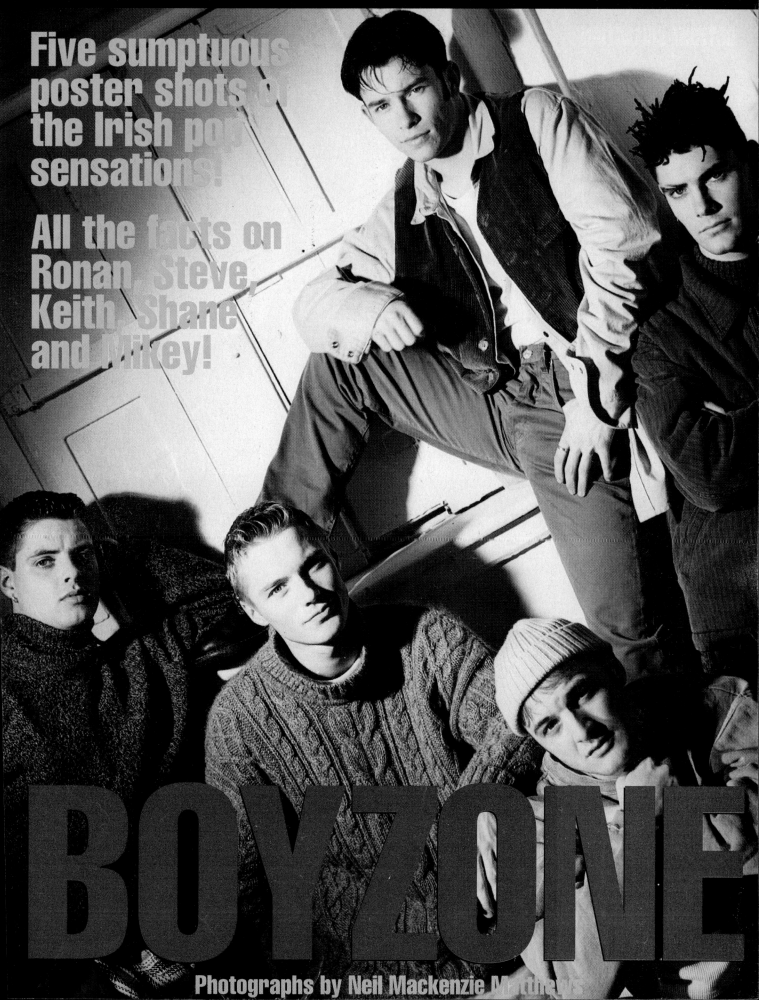

Five sumptuous poster shots of the Irish pop sensations!

All the facts on Ronan, Steve, Keith, Shane and Mikey!

BOYZONE

Photographs by Neil Mackenzie Matthews

RONAN SMASH HITS

BOYZONE COLLECTION

Ronan Keating

Date of birth: March 3, 1977.
Place of birth: Dublin.
Nickname: Tintin – because of his hair.
Body scars/tattoos: None.
Brothers and sisters: Three brothers and one sister, all older. And a nephew (his eldest brother's son) who's also his godchild and is called Conan.
Most valued piece of clothing: Jean Rocher sweater which he hardly ever takes off.
Hero: His eldest brother, Keiran.
Best TV programme: *Quantum Leap.*
Hang-outs: Down the pub! With his folks and his mates.
Big break: Getting into Boyzone after three auditions.
Biggest triumph: Winning the *Smash Hits* Award.
Most embarrassing moment: Forgetting one of his dance moves during a big gig in Dublin – luckily no one seemed to notice!
Most used word/ phrase: Absolutely.
Pets: None.
What his house is like: Quite big and "very mad". Ronan has his own room with a huge bed in it because he "likes his sleep".
Sex life: "Non-existent."
Secret: He was, and still is, a huge Bros fan. His favourite track is *Cat Among The Pigeons.*

Steve Gately

Date of birth: March 17, 1976: "St Patrick's Day".
Place of birth: Dublin.
Nickname: Homeboy – because he used to get homesick.
Body scars/tattoos: A Tasmanian devil tattoo on his hip.
Brothers and sisters: Three brothers (two older) and a sister.
Most valued piece of clothing: Designer cord waistcoat that his parents bought him two years ago for Christmas.
Hero: None.
Best TV programme: *Top Of The Pops.* "It was just amazing when we were on it."
Hang-outs: Round his friends' houses in Dublin or at the cinema.
Big break: Getting into Boyzone after four auditions. *(Although he pretended it only took him three, the same as Ronan!)*
Biggest triumph: Suddenly realising he was famous when people stopped him in the street.
Most embarrassing moment: Dropping the collection box in church and having to pick all the money up off the floor.
Most used word/ phrase: Coooool or reaaaally.
Pets: Sting the dog, a black-and-white shaggy mongrel.
What his house is like: "Homely." When Steve's away his granny stays in his bedroom.
Sex life: "I wish! If something comes up I'll probably take it up."
Secret: He's addicted to Smarties and Jelly Tots.

Keith Duffy

Date of birth: July 1, 1974.
Place of birth: Dublin.
Nickname: Duffster – because of his surname.
Body scars/tattoos: A black panther tattoo on his right shoulder.
Brothers and sisters: Two brothers, aged 20 and 14.
Most valued piece of clothing: His Motorking jacket – he even wears it to bed!
Hero: Johnny Depp.
Best TV programme: *Neighbours* – he's been watching it for years.
Hang-outs: Around Dublin city centre with his mates.
Big break: Winning a *Smash Hits* Award.
Biggest triumph: The award again. "It was an amazing feeling. I never felt so good in my life."
Most embarrassing moment: Running into a shop window in front of loads of fans. "I didn't realise the window was there. I thought it was open. I hit the window and fell to the ground."
Most used word/ phrase: Sorted.
Pets: A rabbit called Hugh and a dog called Socks.
What his house is like: Small with three bedrooms. He shares it with his mum, dad and little brother.
Sex life: "Non-existent. I always plan to start seeing people but whether it happens or not is another story."
Secret: He's short-sighted and he won't tell anybody in case they make him wear glasses.

Shane Lynch

Date of birth: July 3, 1976.
Place of birth: Dublin.
Nickname: Gino – at work he always looked very tanned and they all thought he was foreign.
Body scars/tattoos: Tattoo of a stallion on his shoulder. Scars on his elbow and under his chin from falling off his bike.
Brothers and sisters: Five sisters, two older and three younger.
Most valued piece of clothing: His hats. He's collected over fifty so far.
Hero: His dad.
Best TV programme: *Top Gear* – he loves cars and used to be a mechanic.
Hang-outs: With his family or friends.
Big break: Being picked for Boyzone at the third attempt.
Biggest triumph: "Everything in my whole life is good!"
Most embarrassing moment: An Irish family recognised him in a hotel. He said "hello", then tripped up and fell flat on his face!
Most used word/ phrase: He is the only Irish person who still says, "top of the morning to yer".
Pets: Caesar the snake who eats goldfish.
What his house is like: His mum likes strange things so the hall is paved in stone slabs and one room is like a cave with a rockery and a waterfall... "like a jungle".
Sex life: "None."
Secret: If he can't sleep at night he stays up and scares the other lads!

Mikey Graham

Date of birth: August 15, 1972.
Place of birth: Dublin.
Nicknames: Grahamer – because of his surname.
Body scars/tattoos: Scars on each leg from falling off a roundabout and a wall falling on him. Plus lots of scars on his head... "I was in and out of hospital all the time."
Brothers and sisters: Five sisters and one brother, all older.
Most valued piece of clothing: His Boyzone jacket – even though his name is spelt wrong on it.
Hero: Sting for music, Al Pacino for acting.
Best TV programme: *Top Of The Pops.*
Hang-outs: Round his mates'.
Big break: He was in stage training school and was in a lot of adverts in Dublin. Apparently he had very blond hair and was a sweet little boy!
Biggest triumph: Getting into Boyzone.
Most embarrassing moment: "Meeting everyone at my record company and realising my flies were open."
Most used word/ phrase: You're joking!
Pets: An Old English Sheepdog called Peppy.
What his house is like: Three bedrooms, but his sisters have moved out so there's lots of space for him and his brother.
Sex life: Nothing at the moment. But he's not planning to live a life of "solitude and celibacy".
Secret: He'd rather sing than talk in public, and often stays in when the others are out partying.

Boyzone Fan Club Address: Boyzone, c/o Polydor, 9 White Friars, Aungier Street, Dublin